JESUS OF NAZARETH

THE
HOME UNIVERSITY LIBRARY
OF MODERN KNOWLEDGE

EDITORS OF THE
HOME UNIVERSITY LIBRARY
OF MODERN KNOWLEDGE

RT. HON. H. A. L. FISHER, M.A., F.B.A.
PROF. GILBERT MURRAY, LITT.D., LL.D., F.B.A.
PROF. J. ARTHUR THOMSON, M.A., LL.D.

JESUS OF NAZARETH

By
CHARLES GORE
D.D., D.C.L., LL.D.
FORMERLY BISHOP OF OXFORD

WIPF & STOCK · Eugene, Oregon

Wipf and Stock Publishers
199 W 8th Ave, Suite 3
Eugene, OR 97401

Jesus of Nazareth
By Gore, Charles
ISBN 13: 978-1-60608-264-5
Publication date 11/25/2008
Previously published by Thornton Butterworth, LTD, 1929

CONTENTS

CHAP.		PAGE
	PREFACE	7
I	THE BACKGROUND	18
II	THE GALILÆAN MINISTRY OF JESUS—FIRST PERIOD	41
III	THE TEACHING OF JESUS	91
IV	THE REJECTION AND CRUCIFIXION OF JESUS	128
V	ARE OUR GOSPELS TRUSTWORTHY?	175
VI	THE RISEN JESUS AND THE FAITH OF THE APOSTLES	212
VII	EPILOGUE	249
	AUTHORITIES	254

PREFACE

WHAT I have been invited to do, and have undertaken to attempt, in this volume is obviously a difficult task—to write in about 50,000 words an account of the life and teaching of Jesus of Nazareth to be read by a public which, whatever the divers beliefs of its component individuals may be, will be fairly agreed in demanding a critical history, just as they would demand a critical history of the Buddha or of Socrates. Jesus remains supremely interesting to mankind; but the theories about him and his teaching, and the critical studies of the earliest Christian documents on which these theories are at least professedly based, form to-day a vast literature which it would be impossible to discuss profitably or even to summarize in a small volume. And the attempted reconstructions of the person and teaching of Jesus offered us (for instance) by Renan and Harnack and Wellhausen and Schweitzer and Glover and Middleton-Murry and Henri Barbusse—to say nothing of Papini, who belongs to a different category—are so strangely different from one another, and so seemingly arbitrary in the selection of authentic incidents and sayings on which each in turn is based and the rejection of others which seem to have an equally valid claim for acceptance, that we are tired of these attempts; and certainly I am quite unwilling to add one more to their number. On the other hand it would be useless for me to propound simply the Christ of tradition, Catholic or Protestant. Even one who, like myself, believes that the account of Jesus given by St. Paul and St. John is the true account, and is faithfully safeguarded in the official creed of the Church, must admit that the tradition of the Church (as distinct from its creed) had lamentably obscured the real Jesus by letting men half forget his humanity in its zeal for his divinity, and his example and ethical teaching in its zeal for his atoning sacrifice. That is why Sir John Seeley's *Ecce Homo*—the first and still by far the best of what one may call the humanitarian Lives of Jesus published in English—came upon the orthodox world sixty-three years ago as a terrible shock, simply because of its faithful portraiture of the Man. And still, in spite of the help given by this wonderful book, which every one should read, the task of providing a fairly true and complete image of Jesus, as he lived and as he taught, expressed in modern terms and on a critical basis, fit to be put into the hands of the "average reader" in our country, is very far from being accomplished at present; and my present object is—not to accomplish it indeed, but to further it.

I have felt that the following method would be the most satisfactory. First of all to give by way of introduction an account in outline of the world into which Jesus came. This will occupy Chapter I, and may be taken as fairly uncontroversial and remote from reasonable question. Then I propose to set before my readers the story of Jesus especially as it is given us in the Gospels of St. Mark and St. Luke. (I shall explain later why these Gospels are chosen.) I shall not assume anything about the character of these documents—I mean as so whether, or how far, what they set before us is "the Christ-myth" or is trustworthy history: I shall treat them simply as any historian ought to treat his documents before he begins to pass judgement on them. I shall let them tell their own story. I shall not print the personal pronouns referring to Jesus with a capital letter, because I am assuming nothing, but simply providing such a modern comment on the narratives as shall enable men and women to read again with fresh eyes the two short stories (Mark and Luke) for themselves. Thus Chapter II will interpret their story of Jesus from his first public appearance down to Simon Peter's confession that he was the Christ (Mark i.-viii. 31, Luke iii.-ix. 21). Chapter III will give a fuller account and analysis of the teaching of Jesus—especially on certain points—and in this I shall use also some of the material supplied by St. Matthew. Chapter IV will take up the story of the later ministry, ending in the death of Jesus on the Cross (Mark viii. 32-xv. ; Luke ix. 22-xxiii.). At this point my readers may be taken to be fairly familiar with the earliest story of Jesus which we possess. Then in Chapter V I shall invite them to form at least a provisional estimate of the documents and a provisional conclusion as to their historical trustworthiness. I shall have to content myself with not much more than a reference to the first Gospel and the fourth (St. Matthew and St. John). They must be left in the main for independent study. Then I shall go forward in Chapter VI to trace out how the experience of the first disciples of Jesus up to his death and burial was transformed in the light of their subsequent experiences and became " the Gospel" as we find it in the books of the New Testament generally. I shall attempt to present in barest outline the coherent substance of that Gospel on the basis of which the Christian Church has passed through its manifold developments down to the present day. Finally in the Seventh Chapter, or Epilogue, I shall point out the significance for our own age of the question whether this Gospel of Jesus Christ can still claim to be accepted by a reasonable faith as "the Way, the Truth, and the Life"—the Light to lighten the nations and the strength of the individual soul.

I have thought it better to avoid footnotes almost entirely. A very few have been found necessary—for obvious reasons. But, if there were to be any more, it would be very difficult to restrict them. And I have appended to the last chapter a list of a few of the authorities to be consulted on each chapter separately. I must repeat that I am assuming that the readers of Chapters II, III and IV in this "guide-book" will read for themselves the relevant portions of the Gospels which are referred to in the headings or course of the chapters.

CHARLES GORE.

CHAPTER I

THE BACKGROUND

PALESTINE, the southern portion of Syria (now with Transjordania committed to the government of Great Britain under the mandate), has taken its name, since the days of the Roman Empire, from the Philistines, who had occupied the Mediterranean seaboard before Israel came upon the scene; but it has gained all its importance among the nations from this latter people who, probably in the thirteenth century B.C., occupied its highlands, and who, since the return of the remnant of their race from their captivity in Babylon (from the sixth century B.C.), had come to be known by the name of their chief surviving tribe as the Jews—the people of Judæa. This little people Israel (to call it by its older name) occupying this small territory, roughly about the size of Wales, living moreover in a district where the great Empires clashed—Egypt, Assyria, Babylonia, Persia, Greece, Rome —though constantly, as it seemed, on the verge of extinction or absorption, yet by a sort of miracle of history retained its solidarity and individuality, in spite of frequent disasters and losses, and so maintained its independent spiritual life as finally to become, with Greece and Rome, one of the great factors in the civilization of later Europe and of the lárger world, wherever European peoples have become dominant.

History familiarizes us with the idea of races having specific characters and vocations. Thus in its later intellectual and artistic developments Europe has acknowledged Greece for its mother, and in the arts of law and government Rome; but in the matter of religion the Jews —this appropriation of the religious ideas of the Jews having become possible because their religion lost its narrowness and became universalized through the teaching of Jesus, especially as presented by St. Paul. It was not a vain boast when, about the time of what is called the Conversion of the Empire, the great Alexandrian teacher, Athanasius, declared that, through its prophets, Israel became "the sacred school of the knowledge of God and of the spiritual life for all mankind." It is to these prophets of Israel that we owe, in the main, the ideas of the One God, the creator of all

THE BACKGROUND 15

that is, and of the inseparable union of religion with morality—because the essential character of God is justice and purity, truth and love, and there can be no fellowship with Him or acceptance with Him except by becoming like Him in heart and life. To them also we owe the general idea of mankind as made in God's image, rational, free and responsible, to be His vicegerent upon earth ; and, while grievously sinful and rebellious, yet by the act of God given the opportunity of redemption and recovery, and endowed with the inextinguishable hope of the final victory of God over all rebellious wills or institutions, and the establishment of the Kingdom of God in the whole universe of things.

We live to-day in a world of many opinions, where everything is discussed and doubted, and authoritative dogma is at a discount. But no one can doubt the enormous influence in the whole history of European civilization of these root ideas, nor that it is in the main to the prophets of Israel, of whom the last and greatest was Jesus of Nazareth, that we owe them. The modern man who is disposed to disparage what we call the Old Testament, and to lay stress on its savagery and limitations, had better pause, and taking Dr. Moffatt's translation of the Bible into modern speech, read the

Prophets and the Psalms. He had better pass over and ignore obscure passages, where such occur, which are always of minor importance, and drink in the constant stream of religious and ethical principles, the gradual development of which, over the three centuries of the prophetic succession admits of no mistake. If he goes on to study the Old Testament history, he will find that the religion of Israel had its origin amid barbarous traditions and habits, and quite unethical ideas of God and rites of worship. Plain traces of this rude origin remain in their books. They had been just like the peoples about them, and we see them constantly relapsing upon the old pagan basis: but the prophets, who reckoned their succession from Moses, the great founder of Israel, in both of the two kingdoms into which "the twelve tribes" were divided, were always labouring, by encouragement and denunciation alike, to lift them on to the higher spiritual level which was properly their own, and, after centuries of seeming failure, they won a solid and permanent victory. The remnant of the people who came back from Babylon had accepted the religion of the prophets as their own; and though after a little while they sadly confessed that they had "no prophets more," yet they had got sacred books, to which

THE BACKGROUND 17

henceforth they gave an unconditional allegiance; and these books in different forms embodied the religion of the prophets, both in its idea of God and its idea of the spirit in which the nation and the individual must approach God—" What doth the Lord require of thee, but to do justly, and to love mercy, and to walk humbly with thy God ? "

In earlier days the great prophets finding the cultus, the ceremonial religion, of their people abundantly popular indeed, but quite divorced from morality, had seemed to denounce it and reject it with contempt ; but especially in the books of Deuteronomy and Ezekiel we see a synthesis being accomplished between " the law," both social and ceremonial, and the ethical teaching of the prophets. As has been said, soon after the return of the remnant of the people from the captivity, the succession of the prophets ends. Under the influence of Ezra the Scribe, they then became " the people of the Book " ; and the book was first of all the Law, the five books of " the law of Moses," in which was the codification of various traditions of social and religious obligation, dating back in great part to much earlier and ruder days. The substitution of this written law for the continuous inspiration of prophetic teachers was, as we shall see, attended by serious drawbacks; but this must not be allowed to obscure the fact that at any rate the newly codified law was now permeated by the ethical spirit of the prophets. Later to the Mosaic law was added the collection of the prophetic writings, under which title was included the bulk of the histories, all edited in various degrees in the same ethical spirit. Finally to the law and the prophets was added the Psalms which belonged to the temple worship, and the Wisdom Books (or, as we may call them, the moral philosophy of the Jews) and the apocalyptic book which bore the name of Daniel, with various other books of more ambiguous character. The limit of this third division of the Jewish Bible was not finally fixed in the days of Jesus' life and ministry. But the whole of this collection of Sacred Books—the Bible of the Jews—in the form in which he was familiar with it, was more or less completely penetrated with the spirit of their inspired prophets and, in spite of obvious limitations and survivals of earlier savagery, became the acknowledged basis of his purer and richer teaching.

Compared then with the Greeks we find, on a general review, that the Jews contributed little or nothing to the world's heritage in art or

THE BACKGROUND 19

science; but owing to their idea of the world as the scene of a divine purpose gradually to be realized they greatly enriched the root conception of history; and in the region of religion and morality they became first for Europe, but not only for Europe, the master influence.

Now it is necessary, as far as may be in a very brief résumé, to describe the political and social conditions under which Jesus made his appearance in the Jewish world. We shall be chiefly concerned with the history of the Jews of Palestine, but it must not be forgotten that it was only a small proportion of the scattered race which consented, or had the opportunity, to return to their old home. Long before the first Christian century they had become a widely diffused race, whom we find at the beginning of Christianity exercising a remarkable influence, especially from Babylon in the east, from Alexandria and Cyrene in the south, and from Rome in the west. When Christianity, the child of Judaism, began to spread out into the world, it was the Judaism of " the dispersion " which very largely contributed to its success—even though unconsciously and unwillingly—by having familiarized a considerable section of society with the root ideas of its religion.

But it is with the Jews of the Return, the

Jews of Palestine, that we are chiefly concerned. It was under Persian supremacy that they got their liberty to return; and they lived to themselves, more or less quietly, for more than two centuries till the Macedonian, Alexander the Great, conquered the Persian king at the battle of Issus in 333 B.C. But the consequent Macedonian—that is, Greek—domination did not leave them at all quiet. After Alexander's death there was constant war between the more northerly Greek kingdom of the Seleucids, of which the Syrian Antioch became the capital, and the Southern or Egyptian kingdom of the Ptolemies, to which Palestine at first belonged; and Palestine was largely the scene of the warfare. But what was much more important— Greek civilization and thought became the all-pervading atmosphere of the world to which Palestine now belonged. Later, as a result of the victories of Antiochus the Great, Palestine passed under the Seleucid kings, and Antiochus Epiphanes (175–164 B.C.) made a determined attempt to annihilate the institutions and ideas of Judaism, to prohibit its religion and merge it altogether in the world of Hellenism. The process of Hellenization in its milder forms had had influential support among the Jews themselves, and even among the High Priests, who,

THE BACKGROUND 21

since Ezra, had become the heads of the Jewish State. But the persecution of Antiochus awoke an heroic and fanatical resistance, the leaders of which were found in the priestly family known popularly as the Maccabees, from Judas Maccabæus (which perhaps means " the Hammer "). In all the world's records of successful nationalist uprisings none is more remarkable than this movement, which succeeded in winning again complete independence for Israel over a period of about eighty years (143–63 B.C.) under their priest-kings—kings of the tribe of Levi, not of Judah—of the family of Hasmon. Especially under King Alexander Jannœus the territory of Israel received a wide extension, even on the other side of the Jordan. The Greek cities which had studded Palestine were ruthlessly destroyed; flourishing regions were turned into a wilderness; and the heathen populations in Galilee to the north and Idumæa to the south had already in previous reigns been compelled to submit to circumcision and to become Jews.

At its beginning this movement for the redemption of Israel had its source and strength in the *Hasidim*—that is *the Pious*, the strict observers of the law of Moses and of God. This was the spirit which inspired the Maccabæan martyrs. But it soon appeared that the Hasmonæan kings were turning out to be as brutal, selfish and godless tyrants as any pagans. Thus the Pious, later known as the Pharisees or Separated, were driven into violent opposition to their party. The long struggle between the Pharisees and Sadducees began. The latter name seems to have meant the descendants of Zadok, the high priest under Solomon. Certainly it became the name for the priestly aristocracy with which the Hasmonæan family were now identified. The internal struggle between these two parties became deadly during the rule of Jannœus. When at last he entered Jerusalem in triumph, he had eight hundred of his captives, who were no doubt largely Pharisees, crucified in rows, so that, while he caroused, he might enjoy the spectacle of their dying agonies. It is no wonder that the hatred which the Pharisees felt towards all the representatives of this family was such as to make them ready to welcome even all-conquering Rome from the west, when it appeared upon the field, as preferable at least to the Sadducæan kings.

When, however, the victorious Roman general, Pompey, took and occupied Jerusalem (63 B.C.), though he put an end to the Hasmonæan succession, and the last of these "Kings of the Jews,"

THE BACKGROUND 23

with thousands of his subjects, was carried off to Rome to be exhibited in his triumph, he did not at once bring the Jewish territory under direct Roman control. Rome, in fact, had too many other things to think about. Soon the Roman armies were fighting one another in the civil wars, and a Parthian invasion from the east had overrun Syria and there was need to suppress it. Thus Pompey left Judæa a prey to confusion and bloodshed. The new feature in the situation there was the rise of the Idumræan, Antipater, to power. When finally Rome gave the Jews a king (37 B.C.) it was Antipater's son, Herod, called the Great, Jew by religion, Edomite by race (of the people most of all men hated by the Jews), Greek by sympathies, and Roman by allegiance; and when Octavian in 27 B.C. became the Emperor Augustus, he gave Herod a much enlarged territory.

Herod became in fact a magnificent monarch. He erected the new temple of Jehovah in Jerusalem which was "forty and six years in building" and was one of the wonders of the world. He abolished the lifelong tenure of the high priesthood and brought a family of the old priestly stock—the family of Boethus—from Egypt, out of which he provided at his will a succession of high priests. Generally he patronized Judaism in Jerusalem, but paganism in the Hellenized cities of his realm, and far beyond it. In all directions he was building splendid cities and fortresses and temples to various gods. He had a strong mercenary army of Thracians, Germans, and Gauls. He put to death ruthlessly anyone whom he feared, not least those of his own family. Finally his reign ended in a madness of suspicion and a welter of blood, and he died (4 B.C.) some two or three years after the birth of Jesus.

The Jews had been living under a savage despotism. They sent an embassy to Rome after Herod's death, entreating that they might pass under the direct government of the Emperor. This was their plaint, as Josephus (the Jewish historian) gives it us twice over—" He (Herod) was not a king, but the most barbarous of tyrants who had ever sat on a throne He had slain men innumerable, but the lot of those who survived made them envy those who were slain. He not only slaughtered individuals, but oppressed entire cities. Foreign cities he adorned, but his own he destroyed. . . . So in place of former wealth and good laws, there came utter poverty and lawlessness. In fact the Jews suffered more from Herod than their fathers had suffered since they left Babylon."

THE BACKGROUND 25

Their request for incorporation into the Empire was not however granted at once. Surviving members of Herod's family were appointed, not as kings but with the title of " ethnarch " or " tetrarch," over different parts of his dominions. Rebellions followed, and were suppressed in blood. Two thousand revolting Jews underwent crucifixion at Jerusalem shortly after Herod's death. After nine years Augustus was convinced that there was no alternative to direct government from Rome. So in A.D. 6 Judæa with Samaria was put under a procurator subordinated to the imperial legate for Syria. When the ministry of Jesus began Pontius Pilate was the fifth procurator.

The political situation in Judæa was now this : wherever the procurator chose to assert himself, supported as he was by garrisons in Cæsarea, his head-quarters, and in Jerusalem, his authority was irresistible. But though Pilate from time to time forgot himself, it was not the Roman policy to irritate the susceptibility of the Jews or to interfere with their religion and social life. The temple—which no one who was not a Jew might enter—was left under the control of the " chief priests," assisted by a temple guard of Levites, the subordinates of the priests, and considerable judicial and administrative authority was left in the hands of the sacred council—the Sanhedrin—composed of the chief priests, the elders and the scribes, though the death penalty was (generally at least) reserved to the procurator. There were also minor Jewish councils exercising an inferior jurisdiction at every centre of population. By the "chief priests" (the phrase used in the Gospels) is meant especially the family of Annas. This was perhaps the same family of Boethus which Herod the Great had established in the high-priesthood. The office seems to have remained almost "in commission" among them, the procurator nominating one of them to hold it for a time. When, chiefly through the pressure of this high-priestly family Jesus was put to death, while Caiaphas was actually high priest, his father-in-law Annas appears behind him in control.

Samaria, like Judæa, was under the procurator, but their religious and racial organization was quite independent—the Jews regarding this very mixed race with horror, as something worse than pagans, and they being always ready to retaliate upon any Jews who passed through their territory.

While the Roman procurator was thus established in authority in Judæa and Samaria,

THE BACKGROUND

Herod Antipas was still left as tetrarch in control of Galilee and of the southern district beyond the Jordan (Peræa)—two territories detached from one another—maintaining his own army and collecting his own revenue. Philip also—the one of the Herodian princes who had the best reputation—was left as tetrarch of the northern region beyond the Jordan, including the Decapolis—the ten Greek cities. Both these princes inherited Herod the Great's passion for building—Antipas building as his capital the brilliant city of Tiberias, on the western shore of the Sea of Galilee, which the Jews regarded with special horror as having been built upon an ancient cemetery, and which is never mentioned in the Gospels—Philip refounding and renaming Cæsarea Philippi, thirty miles north of the Sea of Galilee, and building Julias (Bethsaida) at its northern head. It should be noticed that though Galilee in general was the territory of Antipas, the shores of the Sea, or Lake, of Galilee belonged to two jurisdictions, that of Antipas and that of Philip.

This must suffice as a sketch of the political background of the ministry of Jesus : but something must be added about the social conditions of the land and the prevalent religious ideas and parties.

As we have followed even in barest outline the history of Palestine in the last centuries " before Christ," it must have struck us as a horrible record of oppression, revolt, internal division, civil war and brutal reprisals. We have records also of disastrous earthquakes and famines. In spite of the building activities of the Herods, the land must have been full of ruins ; and, as the recent Jewish historian of " Jesus of Nazareth "—Dr. Joseph Klausner— points out, it is natural that it should have become, as the pages of the Gospels describe it, full of disease and especially of nervous and mental disorders. This, he remarks, would have made it a natural seed-plot of Messianic visions of an extravagant kind. It is certainly plain that the land was haunted by the terror of evil spirits, endowed with the fearful power of possessing human bodies. It cannot, however, be said that we get from the Gospels—the documents which alone of those we have give us an intense sense of local colour—the same impression of grinding poverty and misery among the mass of the people as we get in the far-off days of the prophets. There must indeed have been enough selfish luxury in evidence to make the story of Dives and Lazarus strike home, and enough misery and helplessness to justify the

THE BACKGROUND 29

description of the people as " distressed and prostrate, like sheep which have no shepherd." The Epistle of James " the Lord's brother" moreover, if it is authentic, must embody an experience gathered in Palestine over a lifetime, and he has occasion to denounce vigorously enough rich Jewish landowners, as oppressors of the poor. Still, we cannot say that the general effect of the parables of Jesus, which are so full of touches of life, is to suggest widespread misery. We find suggestions there of owners of large properties with their stewards and servants and hired labourers. But the available evidence tends to show that the land was still covered with householders possessing small holdings and living on their own produce. The country in parts, and especially in Galilee, was exceedingly productive and well cultivated; and, even if we reduce immensely Josephus's extravagant figures, Galilee must have been very thickly populated. The Sea of Galilee was moreover rich in fish, and the fish trade was flourishing. In Jewish documents, drawn upon by Klausner, we hear of a vast variety of handicrafts, though the names of the articles manufactured are mostly Greek names and suggest that the trades were largely in foreign hands. On the whole, we need not think of Palestine, for all the awful experiences it had gone through, as a land of destruction and misery. We hear some echo of groans under burdensome taxation both under the Herods and under the Romans. But we have no exact information. All that we know for certain is that the system of farming out the customs, and leaving it to the "publicans" to collect them and make what they could out of them, brought its inevitable consequences in the way of extortion; and that the publicans, higher and lower, were held in detestation among their countrymen. (The direct taxes were collected by Roman officials in the Roman province.) But one feature of the situation must not be forgotten, which was singular and all-important. The Jews, living as they were under an utterly unsympathetic foreign domination, which seemed omnipotent, yet believed that they had a divine right to freedom and more than freedom—and were eagerly expecting the divinely sent Redeemer to raise oppressed Israel to the head of the nations. So it was that the land, and especially Galilee, was always seething with rebellion, and ready to give a welcome to any possible Messiah. The robbers or bandits who infested the wilder districts were, we should suppose, full of "religious" aspirations.

THE BACKGROUND 31

The civilization and commerce of the Greco-Roman Empire must have been well in evidence in Galilee and the neighbouring Decapolis; but while the Jews did business with the Greeks they kept themselves studiously aloof from them; and the atmosphere of the Gospels is as purely Jewish as possible.

This brings us to the consideration of the religious schools or parties among the Jews of the time of Jesus.

The Pharisees, whose origin has been described already, were the class of most importance and held in greatest respect among the Jews generally. Most of the scribes or authorized expounders of the law, with authority to " bind " or " loose " (i.e. prohibit or allow) in matters of conduct, belonged to the Pharisaic party. The basis of their religion was the scriptures, and especially the Mosaic law, as interpreted in the authorized tradition; which, by a system of verbal interpretation which strikes us as quite irrational, had elaborated its requirements till it spread like a net over all the details of human life. The punctilious observance of this elaborated law was their supreme care and their pride. If the common people in their hurried and toilsome lives could not or would not observe it, except in certain points which were commonly regarded as of obligation, they despised them accordingly. " This people that knoweth not the law are accursed." The formalism and legalism of the Pharisees, their self-importance, their unnatural straining of the meaning of their scriptures, interpreted in the light of the denunciation of Jesus under which they fell, have made the Christian world regard them with horror. We must remember, however, that their contemporaries regarded them quite otherwise, and we shall have to reconsider our estimate of them. But some further points about their religious position must be noted. First, their religion was of the Synagogue rather than of the Temple. Partly no doubt through the association of the temple with the hated race of high priests, the Pharisees and the pious Israelites generally, though they observed the feasts, offered the sacrifices and used the temple for private prayer, yet in their thoughts about religion paid more attention to that part of their sacred law which concerned the Sabbath, and generally their social and domestic life— that is to the religion of the synagogue rather than of the temple. The second point to be noted is that the Pharisees attached a special value to certain developments of their religion which begin to appear only in the later books

THE BACKGROUND

of the Old Testament Canon, and which become prominent in the " apocalyptic " books which were not in their Canon at all—such as the belief in the resurrection of the dead, and the elaborated belief in angels and evil spirits. Also their awful reverence towards God had generated a fear of bringing him into any immediate contact with things of the earth. A network of agents and messengers was interposed between man and the supreme and unnameable Jehovah. They talked of " Heaven " rather than of God. Lastly, though they regarded the domination of the pagan and foreigner over Israel with disgust, and confidently expected the promised Messiah, the scion of the House of David, and the Vicegerent of God, to come and liberate Israel and bring in the kingdom of heaven, yet taught by bitter experience, they were resolved to tolerate subjection, to say or do nothing which would be regarded by the Romans as rebellious, and so to devote themselves to the exact observance of the Divine Law as to merit in God's own time the intervention of Heaven.

The old opponents of the Pharisees were the Sadducees. If we take Ecclesiasticus—one of the books of our Apocrypha—as representative of the religion of the Sadducees of a much earlier generation, we should take it to be a rather worldly-wise, gentlemanly religion of a sensible type with a great deal of goodness in it. We will not stop to investigate the differences about providence and freewill, which, according to Josephus, separated them from the Pharisees: nor whether they only accepted as of authority the first division of the Bible—the Books of the Law. Certainly they rejected the Pharisaic tradition which extended and amplified the law with the intention of making a hedge about it, and they rejected the later doctrines of Judaism about the resurrection and about angels and spirits. They were conservatives, who did not want any more religion or religious doctrine than the bare minimum which their fathers had thought necessary. But probably in the eyes of the people generally Sadduceeism was judged not so much by its special tenets as by the fact that its chief representatives at the time of Jesus' ministry were the high priestly house. It was a very wealthy family, drawing its wealth mainly, it would seem, from quite secular sources, and devoted simply to its own interests. Nominally they were priests, having charge of the temple and its sacrifices, but in fact they appear as caring for little but their office, dignity and emoluments, and resolved in every way to keep on good terms with their Roman

THE BACKGROUND

overlords. By them the very mention of a Messiah, as King of the Jews, was regarded with horror as being certain to alarm the Romans. As we shall see, it was they rather than the Pharisees who were mainly responsible for the condemnation of Jesus and insisted upon his execution.

But neither their repudiation of the Messianic hope nor the Pharisaic acquiescence in keeping it in abeyance satisfied the people. Their hearts were full of resentment against the foreign rule, and they were always looking for the Christ to deliver them. Galilee especially teemed with sedition, and the party of the Zealots which gained the upper hand in the last days before the destruction of Jerusalem (A.D. 70) was already in existence. One of the apostles of Jesus had belonged to it.

Josephus in his histories makes a good deal of the presence in Judæa at this period of an ascetic, quasi-monastic, sect of Jews called Essenes. They had an inner circle of celibate devotees and an outer circle of adherents. The brethren dressed in white, practised community of goods and abstained from animal sacrifices and animal food with horror; they attached great importance to constant washings, and they also bound themselves to certain secret doctrines with tremendous oaths. Theirs was apparently a form of Judaism tinctured with Oriental influences. Probably Josephus makes so much of them because he was writing to gratify the Greco-Roman world, and did his best to commend the institutions of the Jews to their taste. Thus, as he compares (rather strangely) the Pharisees to the Stoics, so probably he exaggerates the importance of the Essenes as corresponding to the Pythagoræan brotherhoods. Attempts have been made to represent John the Baptist as an Essene, and Jesus and his disciples as drawing much from them. But they do not appear at all in the Gospels or early Christian books. The resemblances discovered between Christianity and Essenism are not nearly so important as the differences; and we may take it from Dr. Edwyn Bevan that " the idea . . . that Jesus or John came from among the Essenes . . . to-day is left to cranks or writers of fiction." It is of course possible that the first Jerusalem church took hints from them in the matter of communism.

Such was the social and religious background on which Christ appears. It cannot be said that anything in the facts and movements which we have described was at all likely to be fruitful in spiritual revival. But about the year A.D. 26,

THE BACKGROUND

a sudden movement did occur which was in fact the seed-plot of Christianity—that was the movement of John the Baptist. Out of the desert an ascetic appeared, who was clothed like a prophet of old in camel's hair with a leathern girdle about his loins, and whose food was locusts and wild honey. His message, which produced a profound impression, was that the Kingdom of God with its promised King —compared to whom John himself was of no account and was nothing but a herald's voice —was close at hand: but that what ought to have been a message of joy to the Jews, the holy people, was in fact something quite different. Isaiah of old had pictured the terrors of his contemporaries at the very thought of the nearer coming of God—" The sinners in Zion are afraid: trembling hath surprised the godless ones. Who among us shall dwell with the devouring fire? Who among us shall dwell with everlasting burnings?" A cry of consternation of the same kind John sought to awaken from his contemporaries. He denounced their wickedness. They were not fit to welcome the Lord. It was idle for them to boast of being Abraham's seed. They were a generation of vipers. Thus he summoned them to instant repentance, before it was too late—before fearful judgement should fall upon them. For the Christ King, who is coming, will have his winnowing fan in his hand and " he will thoroughly purge his floor and gather his wheat into his garner: but he will burn up the chaff with fire unquenchable." Besides this general message John is represented as giving vigorous moral exhortations to different classes of the community, to the well-to-do, to the publicans, to the soldiers. In all this there is nothing original. John was simply renewing the ethical teachings, the promises and the denunciations of the old prophets. But he also did a new thing. His business was to make ready a people prepared for the Lord—to organize a New Israel to welcome the Christ. With this in view he provided a baptism—a washing or lustration—to be the symbol of a new birth and a fresh start. He bade those who would listen to him to make open confession of their sins, and receive his " baptism of repentance " for their remission in the waters of Jordan. His baptism was indeed of little account, he said, compared with what the Christ would give them when he came. " He shall baptize you with the Holy Spirit." But it sufficed for a preparation.

John produced a deep and wide stirring of hearts, and not only in Judæa, for he brought

THE BACKGROUND

in people from remoter Galilee. Even Herod's conscience was moved by what he heard. Multitudes came to his baptism, though the official scribes and the Pharisees, and no doubt the Sadducees, held aloof. John's disciples became a recognized class or sect whom he had taught to fast and pray; and in later days, when Christianity was spreading, we hear of people as far off as Ephesus who were John's disciples, baptized with his baptism, but knowing nothing of Jesus as the Christ. Later Jesus was to declare that " among them that had been born of women " none was greater than John, that he was more than a prophet, that he was the Elijah whom the prophet Malachi had foretold would precede the coming of the Lord. This is the position which has been always assigned to John in Christian tradition. He was " the Forerunner." In the account of John given by the Jewish historian, Josephus, nothing is said about his announcement of the Christ or his relation to Jesus. For indeed Josephus wrote to conciliate the Roman world, and that at a time when the spread of Christianity was becoming a problem to the Empire, and the Jews found their youngest offspring an immense embarrassment. Josephus found it prudent therefore to say as little as possible about Jesus "reputed to be the Christ." He gives however an account of John " called the Baptist " as a powerful preacher of righteousness, and of his rite of baptism, and of the anxiety which he caused to Herod lest his movement should stimulate rebellion. It was to be beforehand with this possibility, Josephus tells us, that Herod after a while shut up John in prison.

CHAPTER II

THE GALILÆAN MINISTRY OF JESUS

FIRST PERIOD [1]

IT was at the height of the movement inspired by John the Baptist and in close connection with it that Jesus appears on the scene. He came from Nazareth in Galilee, where he had been brought up. He was through his mother Miriam or Mary a second cousin of John and only a few months younger. But the familiar pictures of the Holy Family which represent the two children as brought up together are purely fanciful. It would not appear that Jesus and John had ever met. Their homes were some eighty miles apart—in Judæa and Galilee respectively—and their circumstances had been wholly different. John was a stern ascetic whose life from his youth had been remote from the haunts of men in the wilderness—presumably that terrible region through

[1] See Mark i.–viii. 32 ; Luke iii.–ix. 23.

which the highlands of Judæa sink down abruptly into the awful chasm at the bottom of which, 1,300 feet below sea-level, the Jordan empties itself into the Dead Sea; but Jesus had been reared, and had lived to mature manhood, and had practised the trade of a carpenter, at the loveliest place in Palestine, in the folds of the Galilæan hills, growing in wisdom as in stature and in favour with men and with God. When he came to join the company of John and to receive his baptism—at about the age of thirty—he left behind him his mother —whose husband Joseph was dead—and a numerous group of " brethren " : four brothers are named, besides sisters. Of his childhood we learn nothing, save for one scene, occurring when at the age of twelve he was taken for the first time in company with his parents on the annual pilgrimage to Jerusalem for the Passover Festival, and distressed them by remaining in the Temple after the pilgrims had left the city, absorbed in attention to the teaching of the rabbis. There he appears as a child of extraordinary promise, with so deep a consciousness that God was his Father as to make him independent of all interests except those of learning the ways of God. "Wist ye not," he said to his elders, when they found him and

THE GALILÆAN MINISTRY OF JESUS 43

reproved him—" Wist ye not that I must be in my Father's house " or " in my Father's concerns ? "

A word must be said about his education. He was hailed during his lifetime as a son of David, that is one of the old royal family, and this is alluded to in the New Testament as if it were undisputed. In fact we find in one of the latest documents of the Old Testament (Zechariah xiii. 12) that the men of the family of David with their wives were a recognized group in Jerusalem, and in all probability they would have continued to be so, jealously preserving their real, or supposed, genealogies. If Joseph belonged to this group we should suppose that in the natural course Jewish patriotism, with its deep sense of the divine vocation of Israel, and its glorious Messianic hope, would have been the atmosphere of his childhood and youth. The Sea of Galilee and its neighbourhood abounded in Gentile cities, built under Herodian influences, and Nazareth was near the great plain of Esdraelon, which was the important connecting route, between the East and Egypt and between the East and Rome. Thus cosmopolitan interests and foreign ideas and worships were near at hand to the home of Jesus as he grew. But he appears, like the devout Jews generally, to have been quite untouched by them. During his ministry he never seems to have entered one of the Greek cities, whether Tiberias or Bethsaida or Cæsarea Philippi. " I am not sent," he said, " save unto the lost sheep of the house of Israel." In fact there is not a touch on the Gospel pictures suggestive of foreign influences. He appears to have learnt nothing except what was to be learned from the Jewish Scriptures and in the synagogues, from his own singularly penetrating observation of men and nature round about him, and from communion with his Heavenly Father. But what he learned from outside was as nothing compared to what he learned from within. He was profoundly original. His interpretation of the Scriptures diverged, as we shall see, widely from that of their authorized expositors, the scribes or " lawyers." It comes to us, as we study it, like a breath of fresh air. No doubt John the Baptist had already been reviving the ethical spirit of the old prophets of Israel as against the Pharisaic legalism. That was a link which bound Jesus to John. But the intuition of Jesus into the purpose and drift of the Old Testament was far more profound and novel than anything we can attribute to John.

THE GALILÆAN MINISTRY OF JESUS 45

All we can say then about the education of Jesus is that it was a thoroughly and exclusively Jewish education, to which the spirit of Jesus reacted, in one sense, with whole-hearted acceptance—in the sense that he embraced with a profound conviction the prophetic faith in Jehovah, the God of Israel, as the one and only God, the Creator of all that is, and the belief that God had called Israel to be in a special sense His people, and had given Israel its mission to the nations, and its sacred law, and through the prophets had given to it the assurance of the good time coming when God's reign on earth should be realized in Israel and should spread from Israel to the nations of the earth. It is quite impossible to interpret Jesus of Nazareth with any reality except on the basis of this assurance. What drew him to John the Baptist was no doubt the rumour pervading the whole land that a new prophet had arisen who declared that after age-long delays this Kingdom of God or Kingdom of Heaven— this coming of God into His own in judgement and in mercy—was now immediately at hand.

So Jesus went the four days' march from Nazareth down into the Jordan Valley near where it issues into the Dead Sea, and after all the people seeking baptism had been baptized he too was baptized, seemingly alone. But with him it was not an occasion for the confession of sins and reception into the New Israel, but for divine recognition and divine mission. " He saw the heavens rent asunder and the Spirit as a dove descending upon him; and a voice came out of the heavens, Thou art my only Son (that is the true meaning of the word translated ' beloved ' in our Bible), in thee I have found satisfaction." We need not suppose that the vision and the voice were a spectacle which would have been seen and a sound which would have been heard by an indifferent spectator: more probably they were like the visions and voices which came to the old prophets. But if we are to understand truly anything about the mission of Jesus we must recognize that at that moment he received with unhesitating conviction the assurance of his divine vocation as the Messiah and the power to fulfil it.

This decisive moment in the life of Jesus was followed by a forty days' solitude with fasting in the awful " wilderness " already referred to. (Jewish like Arabic arithmetic was not at all mathematical, and " forty " does not mean anything much more definite than " many.") " The Spirit driveth him forth

THE GALILÆAN MINISTRY OF JESUS 47

into the wilderness, and he was in the wilderness tempted of Satan." The account of the temptation which is given to us in St. Matthew's and St. Luke's Gospels, if it is a real history (and who can well doubt it?) must have been communicated by Christ to his disciples. We shall probably agree with the great third-century scholar, Origen, that the incidents described in the Temptation narrative—the carrying of Jesus up to the pinnacle of the Temple and again up into the "exceeding high mountain," where were spread out under his eyes "all the kingdoms of the world and the glory of them"—were not external occurrences; but that Jesus thus represented, as in a parable, to his disciples, what were really inward experiences of his soul—powerful and vivid images. The three temptations, so conceived, represent not so much the temptations of the ordinary man as the typical temptations of the exceptional man, whose soul is possessed with a sense of a divine vocation which absorbs his whole interest. And the temptations are even more special and unique than this would imply. They have no meaning except for one who had become conscious of exceptional—what we call miraculous—powers in nature—one who felt he could turn stones into bread, and call upon God to protect him if he cast himself down from the "pinnacle of the Temple"; and one, again, to whom the vision of world-wide sovereignty, in some sense, represented no ridiculous impossibility.

Thus it was that Jesus found himself there in the wilderness tempted to supply his urgent physical needs by turning stones into bread, and repudiated the temptation by appealing to a text from the book of Deuteronomy which recalled how God provided food for his hungry and resourceless people in another wilderness, without any effort of theirs. So if a man would but throw himself on the word of God—would "seek first the Kingdom of God and his righteousness"—his natural necessities would be provided for. This we find was the law of his whole life and the principle which he inculcated on his disciples during his mission. He absolutely refused to use the "power which went out of him" to supply his own needs. The mocking cry addressed to him on the cross expressed the truth—"He saved others, himself he cannot save." When we reflect upon the scandals which have disfigured Church history, because the ministers of religion have misused their spiritual vocation to "feather their own nests," we understand the force of

THE GALILÆAN MINISTRY OF JESUS 49

the temptation and the meaning of Jesus' stern rejection of it. The next temptation was to what we may call thaumaturgy—to dazzle men's imagination by portents of power, such as flinging himself from a lofty height in reliance upon supernatural support, for which the devil quoted scripture. Jesus was constantly tempted in this way by the demands that he would show the people a "sign." But this suggestion he met by another text from Deuteronomy. It would be to "tempt God," not to rely upon Him. Here we get another law of Jesus' ministry. He made a very moderate use of his extraordinary power and gave it a subordinate place. He refused to use it for display, but kept it as an instrument of divine compassion to be used under the guidance of prayer. The story of Jesus is singularly unlike the records of thaumaturgy in general. Finally came the temptation of the exceeding high mountain and the vision of the Kingdoms of the World, It was the temptation to win the world by accepting the service of Satan—that is, by using the ways of the world. That has been the constant temptation of the ecclesiastic, in high position or low, and of the statesman or reformer—the temptation moreover constantly yielded to—which Jesus met by another appeal to Deuteronomy—to its assertion that the service of God is an exclusive service which leaves room for no divided allegiance. That it is impossible to serve God and Mammon Jesus declared to his disciples, and it was the constant principle of his own life. No breath of worldliness—no appreciation of wealth or "respect of persons" ever sullied it.

We cannot reasonably imagine that among the first disciples in the church at Jerusalem there would have been one with the spiritual imagination necessary to invent such an account of the initial temptations of Jesus in the wilderness as is here given us. They are temptations so unusual, and yet so deeply congruous with the unique situation of the subject of them, exhibiting so deep an insight into his character and so summary a disclosure of the laws of his life and actions, that it is hard indeed to doubt that the account is authentic. With the credibility of the miraculous power which Jesus believed himself, and was believed by the people, to possess, we are not yet concerned. We shall return to that question later on. We are now only concerned to tell the story of Jesus as the Gospels—especially St. Mark and St. Luke—put it before us.

In both of these Gospels the baptism and the temptations are followed immediately by the Galilæan ministry which Mark describes as consequent upon the capture and imprisonment of John by Herod Antipas. But we must just notice the correction of the story supplied by the Gospel according to St. John. Here we have a whole series of events expressly dated before John was cast into prison. In Mark and Luke, the Baptist announces himself as the immediate forerunner of the Christ —one much greater than himself, "the lachet of whose shoes I am not worthy to stoop down and unloose"; but nothing is said of any recognition by John of Jesus as being the Christ. The first Gospel, however, implies this, and the last makes it very explicit and describes the passage of some of John's disciples (whom we afterwards find among the apostles) from his school to that of Jesus, whom they too recognize as "the King of Israel." There follows a preliminary self-announcement of Jesus at Cana of Galilee and at Jerusalem, and then a period during which Jesus and his disciples carried on in Judæa a ministry of baptism like John's, and in his neighbourhood. The relation of the story of the Fourth Gospel to that of the others is a question full of difficulty and we shall not find room for it in this little book. But the recognition of Jesus by John as the coming Christ, and at least the close association of the two before John's imprisonment, are almost necessary to explain the story as it is given in St. Mark and St. Luke. Something of the sort is implied in the later intimate references to the Baptist which we find ascribed to Jesus in their narratives, and his " Gospel of the Kingdom " was directly continuous with the preaching of John. It is also more probable that the call of the first disciples was not so abrupt a proceeding as it would there appear to be.

Before he was taken prisoner John must have moved over the Jordan into Herod Antipas's dominions. This step was most probably taken to avoid the opposition of the Pharisees, which would have been less strongly felt on the other side. But in fact he found there a no less formidable opponent. Herod's antagonism to John is ascribed by the Jewish historian Josephus to his fear that he would excite a rebellion. It is ascribed by Mark to the hostility of Herodias, Herod's brother's wife, whom Herod had married in spite of John's denunciation—
" It is not lawful for thee to have thy brother's wife." Herodias, in revenge, wanted to kill him;

THE GALILÆAN MINISTRY OF JESUS

but Herod, who respected him, would do no more than shut him up and keep him safe. The two causes suggested by Josephus and the Evangelists respectively are not incompatible. At any rate, John's public mission was brought to an end by his imprisonment in the fortress of Machœrus; and Jesus, already convinced that he would find no fair hearing in Jerusalem or in Judæa, " withdrew " to Galilee, where the population was much thicker and opportunities were more open, and to the Sea of Galilee, whither his family moved away from their old home at Nazareth, settling in Capernaum on the shores of the lake, which was also the home of several of the first disciples. So we are introduced to the story of Jesus' ministry in Galilee upon which St. Mark and St. Luke focus our attention.

The message of John had been, as we have seen, that the blessed time promised—the Kingdom of God to be realized in Israel—was now at hand, and Israel must prepare to welcome it by a profound reformation; for at present they were quite unfit for it, and it could come upon them only as a judgement. This message Jesus reiterated, but with a marked change of accent. The Kingdom was not only " at hand ": it was, it appeared, already among men in virtue of his coming. He did not indeed talk about himself: he made no proclamation of Messiahship. He called himself the "Son of Man." This phrase will need some further discussion, but it is fairly evident that as used by our Lord from the first it was a quite non-committal title. It probably meant no more than "the man"—though, as when in the Old Testament the prophet Ezekiel was constantly so addressed, it meant "the man" in some special sense and with some special commission. However, in his coming the Kingdom had come. What prophets and kings of old had desired to see and hear, but had been disappointed, was now the happy portion of the disciples of Jesus: John the Baptist for all his greatness had been outside the Kingdom, but the meanest disciple was inside; it had "come upon" men and if they had eyes to see it, they would find it among them. The preaching of Jesus began thereon a jubilant note. Invited at the synagogue in Nazareth to read and expound the scriptures he had read the forecast given by the Second Isaiah of the Servant of Jehovah, "The spirit of the Lord is upon me, because he anointed me to preach good tidings to the poor: he hath sent me to proclaim release to the captives, and recovery of sight to the blind, to set at liberty them that are bruised, to proclaim the acceptable year of the Lord." He stopped there—omitting the note of judgement in the ancient text " and the day of vengeance of our God." The first preaching was to be simply " words of grace " addressed to the poor and oppressed. It has been customary to explain the similar words, " Come unto me, all ye that labour and are heavy laden, and I will give you rest; for my yoke is easy and my burden is light," as addressed to those who feel the burden of *sin*: but this is gratuitous. The soul of Jesus was filled with an infinite pity for the poor and bewildered people of Galilee whom he saw as sheep which had no shepherd. And he told them that, if they would trust him and his message, the good time promised them by the prophets would be found to have come. God was their Father who loved them each and all with a father's love, and he was sent to speak to them in the Father's name. The tidings of great joy had at last come to the poor.

And the people listened: they felt in this new teacher a marvellous authority which made them trust him. They had lived like the rest of the world, in terror of malignant spirits;

and lunacy, which they took as a sign of "possession," abounded in their towns and villages. Jesus, it appeared, would have men still believe that their lives are really surrounded and influenced by spirits favourable and hostile. But he would have those who trusted their Father in heaven cease to fear the malignant spirits; and what impressed the people more than anything else was the absolute control he had over them and their terror in his presence—that is the terror of the possessed persons. But he was seen also to exercise a wonderful control in the whole kingdom of nature. A centurion—that is, an officer in the troops of Herod—who was friendly to the Jews, though not a Jew himself, was so deeply impressed by his powers that he sent humbly to implore him to heal his favourite servant, who was dying. He explained that he had not ventured to approach him himself, nor did he ask him to come to his house. But as an officer in the army he knew what delegated authority meant, and the power of the officer's mere word: and he recognized that Jesus held such delegated authority from God that his bare word could heal his servant. Something like this was no doubt the common impression. When Jesus taught, it was " not as the scribes "

THE GALILÆAN MINISTRY OF JESUS 57

with elaborate proofs and appeals to authorities : it was as one who had authority in himself to speak, and could justify his speech by a like authority to control all harmful forces. So when the paralysed man was brought in his helpless condition by his friends, and they showed their faith by overcoming the obstacles which hindered their approach to Jesus, letting him down through the roof on his bed in front of him, Jesus first assured the man of the forgiveness of his sins, and when the Pharisees murmured at this, " Who can forgive sins but God only ? " he justified his assumption of spiritual authority by healing the man—" That ye may know that the Son of Man hath power on earth to forgive sins." This is the first impression he gave in Galilee—an impression of authority as well miraculous as moral ; and in the crowded district full of misery it produced a widespread popular movement of enthusiasm for the new prophet and teacher. " God," they cried, " hath visited his people ! "

That is the first impression we get from the story of the Galilæan ministry. Alike the sick and the miserable and all the humble folk who cherished at heart the hope of Israel that God would one day " visit and redeem his people " felt in the presence of Jesus the kindling of a new faith. A wide-spreading joy and hope traversed a region of the earth which had known so much cruelty and misery. The Kingdom, the vision of which Jesus spread out before them, was a kingdom of healing, health and love, based on the assurance that God was their Father, loving every one individually with the same love, because every soul in His sight was of infinite worth and every penitent sinner would find with Him the readiest welcome and the freest forgiveness. Such teaching found ready access to their hearts. Jesus claimed indeed of men an absolute and childlike faith in his word and power. Where there was no such faith he could do nothing. At Nazareth, for instance, we read " he could do no mighty works " and " he marvelled because of their unbelief." But this initial faith in his power and goodness arose widely and spontaneously— " The common people heard him gladly " and " all men sought him," and multitudes were healed as Jesus passed on circuit through the large villages of Galilee.

Of course this sort of belief in the new prophet was largely engendered by his wonderful powers, and was not more than what is called in the Gospels " a faith to be healed." But from the first it was the intention of Jesus to

THE GALILÆAN MINISTRY OF JESUS 59

organize an inner circle of " disciples." We find objectors to Jesus talking about " thy disciples " as a recognized group, like the " disciples of John " or " the disciples of the Pharisees "; and very early we find Jesus " calling " certain men away from their businesses to be constantly " with him." The stories of their calls and eager responses are very vivid and familiar. Twelve especially were chosen, of whom Simon, renamed by Jesus Peter (Rockman), was the leader, and with him were his brother Andrew and two other fiery spirited fishermen, James and John the sons of Zebedee —nicknamed Boanerges or Sons of Thunder— and Philip and Bartholomew. All these, as we gather from the fourth Gospel, (except James) had come out of John the Baptist's fellowship. Besides these were Levi (or Matthew) the publican, and another James, probably his brother, and Thomas and Simon the Zealot, and Judas Iscariot, who alone seems to have come from Judæa. The twelfth—another Simon—left no memorial but his name, which indeed is variously given. These twelve men were appointed the agents of Jesus and were sent out as " apostles " in the service of the Kingdom and the New Israel. Though Jesus made no public announcement of Messiahship, the appoint-

60 JESUS OF NAZARETH

ment of such legates was an official act on his part, as when the Sanhedrin at Jerusalem sent apostles abroad to collect the Temple tribute. The disciples of Jesus were thus already a recognized group and they found their centre in the Twelve.

Thus the movement of Jesus had an enthusiastic and successful beginning in Galilee and it was a movement full of joy. When Jesus was questioned as to why he did not, like the Pharisees or John, institute fasts for his disciples, he replied by comparing them to the enthusiastic companions of a bridegroom on the occasion of his marriage, who for the time have forgotten all other interests in their zeal to do honour to their companion. "How shall the children of the bride chamber fast while the bridegroom is with them?" If he added some words about "days to come" which would have a very different character, they were added as it were in an undertone and passed without comment.

But the success of the appeal of Jesus was not unchequered even at the outset. When John in his prison was troubled with doubts whether this Jesus was really "he that should come," and sent disciples to ask him the direct question, he (as usual) gave no direct answer.

He bade them tell John of the wonderful works of mercy which they saw or heard of, and of the preaching of the good tidings to the poor. But he added, " Blessed is he whosoever shall not be offended in me." It is these original causes of offence that we must examine.

We find recorded his failure at Nazareth, where in the Sabbath service in the synagogue he had read the glorious prophecy of the Second Isaiah, as has been already mentioned, and claimed its fulfilment in himself. Some had wondered reverentially at his " gracious words," but the majority of the villagers had been scandalized at this familiar person, just one of themselves, making such a claim. He had offended them besides by giving Capernaum a seeming priority over his own native village in healing the sick, and he did not remove that offence by reminding them that former prophets had been sent not to their own people but to foreigners, and that their own homes were the last places likely to welcome them. Thus at Nazareth he got a very rough reception and could do nothing. This, however, was exceptional, but the evidence of a much deeper and more widespread opposition very soon began to appear. It arose among the " people of position " in the community, and no wonder !

The Son of Man showed a profound respect for *any* man or woman. No one could fail to see that his idea of mankind was exalted indeed. But his sense of the infinite worth of a human soul was apparent especially in his dealings with those whom public opinion discredited or hated or found repulsive—customs-officers, harlots, lepers, Samaritans. He was equally friendly indeed to Pharisees who welcomed him. But he had no respect of persons. Whatever gave people in their own eyes the title to be regarded as superior persons, and to look down on others or exploit them in their own interests, he viewed with a disgust of which he made no concealment, even at the tables of the rich. Thus he hated the accumulation of property, as such. He spoke of money (*mammon* in the language of Palestine) as a rival god or false idol, to worship which is to dethrone the true and only God. He regarded riches as almost necessarily excluding from the Kingdom. In the parable of the Rich Fool he poured contempt upon pride of possession. In the parable of Dives and Lazarus he unmasked the dining-room of the rich man as the vestibule of a place of torment in Hades. Plainly avarice, or the desire for more and more money, or the estimate of money-making as the end in life, was at least

THE GALILÆAN MINISTRY OF JESUS 63

as bad in his eyes as lawless lust or any disreputable sin. Naturally therefore the well-to-do, not indeed without exception but for the most part, regarded this new teacher who was gathering crowds of disciples with aversion or with an assumption of contempt which was ill-concealed fear.

Among the Jews, however, it would really seem that the knowledge of God was more thought of than wealth. Their natural tradition made it of much more importance. And the Pharisees were thus the people of most importance in society. But religion in their minds was identified with the maintenance of "the tradition" in the light of which alone the scriptures could be rightly interpreted; and of that tradition they were the guardians. A high esteem of themselves in their capacity as leaders had become identified in their minds with religion. They had already become very restive under the teaching of John the Baptist, but in the teaching of Jesus things had become much worse. Jesus indeed believed in the Word of God as spoken by the Prophets and in the Law given by God, and he bade the people respect its authorized interpreters who "sat in Moses' seat." None the less, his teaching was revolutionary. He found that the official teachers had made the Word of God of none effect by their tradition. He on his part demanded that the Law should be interpreted in terms of the prophets. He kept quoting Hosea, "I have desired mercy and not sacrifice." Against all their system of minute prescriptions he exalted the great moral principles. He "purged all meats" by finding the seat of pollution only in the heart of man. He constantly offended them by healing the sick on the Sabbath Day or by countenancing his disciples in what they regarded as laxity in its observance. "The Sabbath," he said, "was made for man and not man for the Sabbath : wherefore the Son of Man is Lord also of the Sabbath." Nor could it be denied that he claimed a power to supersede even the written law, as if it were imperfect, and as if he could, of the authority which his Father had given him, go farther and deeper in proclaiming the will of God. He described his doctrine as a "new wine" which could not be put into the "old bottles" of the tradition. It ought to be added that Jesus' constant habit of speaking of God under the familiar name of "Father"—"My Father" or "Your Father" —would not have had an agreeable sound in the ears of those who, in accordance with what

THE GALILÆAN MINISTRY OF JESUS 65

was already ancient tradition, did not dare to name God at all, but preferred to speak of "the heavens."

It was then obvious to the Pharisees (of whose party were the majority of the official "scribes" or "lawyers") that the influence of Jesus would discredit them and their order. Here was a young man—in their eyes a mere layman—bidding them, the authorized teachers of religion, to think again about the whole meaning of their religion, to acknowledge vast mistakes which they had made and to imbibe a doctrine which was indeed a "new wine." It is rare indeed in history to find the authorities of any old-established church of whatever kind ready to meet such a challenge with anything but unmitigated hostility. So they declared war against him; and Jesus treated them finally as "blasphemers of the Spirit" manifested in his mission—as enemies of the Light Divine. When we find Jesus speaking with joy of his experience that it was simple or ignorant people, not the wise and learned, who welcomed his preaching, we must remember of what sort the "learning" of Israel was. It was verbal familiarity with the Law of Moses mixed with the tradition of the scribes, who had expanded and interpreted its provisions so as to cover the whole of life with an infinitely detailed system of prescriptions. They had thus made themselves masters of a highly specialized "science" of interpretation which would seem to us the very negation of all real science, but which sufficed at least to exclude the claim of any unauthorized person to interpret the scriptures for himself, or to let in the light into the dungeon of tradition. These learned men were in a sense very conscientious—with a very exacting standard of positive duty: but they stood for keeping the saving knowledge in their own hands. It was this sort of knowledge—the knowledge which entitles a select few to despise others and warn them off their own preserves—which Jesus hated as he hated selfish wealth. "Woe unto you lawyers (or scribes)," he said later in his life, "for ye have taken away the key of knowledge: ye neither entered in yourselves, and those that would enter in ye hindered." Of genuine knowledge, all that can really be called light in whatever department of life, there is no sign of depreciation on the part of Jesus, though he never appears himself as teaching anything except religion. No great teacher in fact—not even Socrates—ever believed more profoundly in the average man's capacity for thinking, or insisted more fully on his exercising his capacity.

THE GALILÆAN MINISTRY OF JESUS 67

His refusal to give plain answers to plain questions —his constant habit of dealing with one question by asking another—was, we should gather, part of a general refusal to teach explicitly and dogmatically, lest he should thereby stunt a man's capacity for finding his own answers to his own questions by the light given him within. We must remember this when we hear Jesus saying, " I thank thee, Father, Lord of heaven and earth, because thou hast hid these things from the wise and prudent and has revealed them unto babes." It was another instance of his hatred of any human claim to such exclusive advantages as would enable a select few to despise or look down upon the mass of men as inferior persons.

Again, wherever there is a privileged class, it takes it as a matter of course that those outside its charmed circle are to regard it as their vocation to minister to their superiors. They exist to be exploited for the advantage of the few. Now, Jesus was no " equalitarian." He showed no objection to the existence in society of a hierarchy of orders. In his own new society, as we shall see, he established a body of officers, clothed with authority. But in his view these " superiors " were to consider themselves only as persons destined to a particular and more exacting kind of service. He said to the selected apostles, " The kings of the Gentiles have lordship over them, and they that have authority over them are called Benefactors : but it shall not be so among you. But he that is greater among you let him become as the younger ; and he that is chief as he that doth serve ; even as the Son of Man came not to be ministered unto but to minister, and to give his life a ransom for many." There was a fund of fiery indignation in the heart of Jesus which from time to time blazed out in a fierce denunciation. Against no persons or actions did it blaze so fiercely as against those who exploited the weak and helpless for their own pleasure or profit. " It is not the will of your Father that is in heaven that one of these little ones should perish." " Woe unto the man through whom the offence cometh. It was better for him that a millstone were hanged about his neck and that he should be drowned in the depths of the sea." In a world used to the idea of slavery, even in the Jewish world into which the prophetic teaching had infused a certain sense of the spiritual equality of all Israelites, but not of the spiritual equality of all men, the sort of teaching which Jesus gave was revolutionary ; and it was natural that rich men and owners of property

THE GALILÆAN MINISTRY OF JESUS 69

and the holders of religious authority should listen to it with pretended scorn and secret terror.

Society was freer, the spiritual atmosphere was more open, in northern Galilee than in southern Judæa : and it was, no doubt, for this reason that after the capture and inprisonment of John, Jesus had begun his mission, or begun it afresh, in Galilee. But very soon he found himself under observation. " There were scribes and doctors of the law from Jerusalem (especially) sitting by." A deputation was there to watch him and to report. No doubt the Pharisees of Jerusalem, from whom they came, were, in a way, nearer in their aims to Jesus than any other class. They were more devoted than any other class to the interests of religion. But they had such a false or one-sided idea of religion— one so bound up with the sense of their own importance—that Jesus was more obnoxious to them than to any other class, and they fell finally under his sternest denunciations.

There is another point which we must notice in this connection. In every settled society there tends to grow up a distinction between respectable and disreputable sinning. Certain kinds of sins are " scandalous." They tend to upset the decent order of society; they " outrage morality," by which is meant the accepted standard of orderly and decent living. Such sins are murder and violence and theft, and blasphemous or atheistical language, and adultery or open sensuality which desecrate the home life. Other sins, though they may be formally regarded as sins, are tacitly condoned or taken for granted. Now, no one can read any one of the Gospels without perceiving that Jesus absolutely refused to recognize any such distinction between respectable and disreputable sins. Nothing is more evident than that in his eyes the love of money, selfishness, contempt of others, pride, uncharitableness, are at least as bad as violence or adultery or fornication. Nay, he regarded the sins which are scandalous in the eyes of society as in this sense less spiritually dangerous than the respectable sins, that the latter are harder to repent of and to forsake. " The publicans and the harlots," he said to the highly respectable Pharisee, " go into the Kingdom of God before you." " How can ye believe," he asked them, " who receive honour one of another, and the honour that cometh from the only God ye seek not ? " None, he meant, are so hide-bound as those who live, and are content to live, by the standards of a close society. No close society known to history has ever accepted a more exacting standard

THE GALILÆAN MINISTRY OF JESUS 71

than the Pharisees: and for that very reason it was the most hide-bound.

No doubt some writers, not only in our own age, have misused the fact that Jesus was specially alive to the danger of "respectable" sins, as if it meant that he was lenient or comparatively indifferent to those which are commonly " disreputable "—in particular that he condoned or lightly regarded sexual sin. But this is not the case. He refused to regard any class as hopeless—not even " publicans " (who were loathed as enemies of their own people and were no doubt in fact a bad class) nor harlots. He found more penitent converts among them than amongst the Pharisees, and he gave them ready absolution. Apparently he very seldom talked about sexual sin. He looked to the " expulsive power of a new affection "—a new direction given to all the faculties of the human soul— to restore supremacy to the spirit over the flesh. But when he did talk about sensual sin, it was with a simple severity. One of the few occasions when he gave a plain answer to a plain question and spoke with dogmatic authority was in asserting the indissolubility of the marriage tie. On the same occasion he gave a special place of honour to the celibate vocation, and on another occasion he demands the sternest

72 JESUS OF NAZARETH

discipline of sexual thoughts and desires as well as outward actions, and bade men prefer even a maimed or hampered life to a life of sensual " freedom " ; because even a maimed life is better than total ruin, and sensual indulgence is an open road to total and final ruin. It is also noticeable that he chose his agents—his " apostles "—exclusively, as it would appear, among respectable, well-to-do men of the working class, though he proceeded to subject them to a training so deep and searching as left no place within them for the pride which clings to respectability. The hysterical or " abandoned " men and women, whom he healed and absolved and inspired with a new devotion—of the sort who would be most easily liable to religious enthusiasm—he seems to have refused to take into his company of agents, but sent back to their homes.

On the whole as we read the story of Jesus it is obvious, and ought never to have been left out of sight, that the Gospel of the Kingdom, as Jesus preached it in Galilee, was pre-eminently a Gospel for the poor and the oppressed, and was such as would naturally have been found " offensive " first of all to the rich, and to the highly respected leaders of religion, and generally to the privileged classes and their adherents.

THE GALILÆAN MINISTRY OF JESUS 73

The secular authority over Galilee, when Jesus was preaching there, was the petty prince or tetrarch, Herod Antipas. As we have seen, he had imprisoned John the Baptist when he had come preaching and baptizing into Peræa, partly probably from fear of a " democratic " movement. And we are not surprised to find him and his adherents suspicious of Jesus. So we notice the Herodians joined with the Pharisees in a determination to silence this troublesome voice.

Before passing away from this aspect of Jesus' teaching we must not fail to notice his attitude towards women. There was a good deal in the sacred literature of Israel tending to give a high status to women, but on the whole it would be true to say that they were still treated as the chattels and instruments of men. Contemptuous references to womankind can easily be quoted from the Old Testament and the Rabbis ; Jesus showed no disposition to include women among his apostles or official agents : but he constantly treated women as of the same spiritual worth as men. He is represented as talking freely to them in public places contrary to the Jewish custom. When he had to do with " fallen women " he totally refused to treat them with contempt or under a " taboo." He welcomed their repentance and set them free. In his ministry of mercy he showed the same regard to women as to men. For a part of his ministry at least a company of women was attached to the company of the disciples and ministered to them of their substance. Women, like Martha and Mary, were among his friends and he thought them worthy of his highest teaching. He saw in them, that is, the same spiritual worth and capacity as men. It was in the same spirit that he took a special pleasure in calling attention to good actions on the part of Samaritans. He would honour *all* men.

Galilee was not an aristocratic district, and, as we have seen, the first preaching of Jesus was received there with enthusiasm. " The common people heard him gladly." " All men seek thee," his disciples told him. This was natural—but we have now to consider what checked his movements among the mass of the people, and we shall find that the causes of this check, which became what observers must have called total failure, were chiefly two.

First let us consider Jesus' absolute refusal to use or countenance the use of force. In face of the world he seemed to demand of his followers deliberate and unlimited submission to wrong or injustice: " I say unto you that hear, love

THE GALILÆAN MINISTRY OF JESUS 75

your enemies, do good to them that hate you, bless them that curse you, pray for them that despitefully use you. To him that smiteth thee on the cheek offer also the other; and from him that taketh away thy cloke withhold not thy coat also. Give to every one that asketh thee; and of him that taketh away thy goods ask them not again. . . . If ye do good to them that do good to you, what thank have ye? For even sinners do the same. And if ye lend to them of whom ye hope to receive, what thank have ye? Even sinners lend to sinners, to receive again as much. But love your enemies, do them good, and lend, never despairing (or 'hoping for nothing again'); and your reward shall be great, and ye shall be sons of the Most High: for he is kind toward the unthankful and the evil. Be ye merciful even as your Father is merciful."[1] We shall have to come back upon this teaching when we are considering the use Jesus made of proverb, paradox, and parable. But we must not explain it away. We must take it as illustrated by his own example. Whatever powers of resistance he believed to be at his disposal, he refused to use them. At the last he said, "He that taketh the sword shall perish by the sword," and he yielded him-

[1] Luke vi. 27–36.

self passively, the just to the unjust. "He was led as a lamb to the slaughter." So he prepared his disciples to act when he sent them out defenceless into a hostile world.

But by such an attitude of passivity under injustice, he no doubt alienated a very large class of persons in Galilee. For Galilee was seething with discontent, and every "false Christ" who arose between this period and the destruction of Jerusalem in A.D. 70, could reckon upon finding followers reckless enough, if only they might have their fling, and take their chance of breaking the hated foreign yoke. The form of Messiahship which would have appealed to them would have been the militant form which the Old Testament abundantly suggested. The Pharisees indeed urged submission to the Romans for the present. It was, they held, useless to resist. One day, if they kept the law faithfully and scrupulously, God would act for them and bare his arm to overthrow their enemies. The more fiery spirits were no doubt already impatient under this teaching. But Jesus' teaching was worse. He seemed to look forward to no splendid movement, such as would recall and surpass the glories of the Maccabees. If at one moment they fell under the spell of Jesus—if they would

THE GALILÆAN MINISTRY OF JESUS 77

have come by force and made him a king, that must have been because they thought that they could force him to throw off his mask, to use his magnificent power to fight for Israel and " wash his footsteps in the blood of the ungodly." But he fled from them, and they gave him up. No doubt also they resented what they would have called his lack of patriotism—that he was kind to such enemies of Israel as Samaritans and publicans. We can imagine that the position of Simon the Zealot among the apostles must have been a very difficult one, and must have involved a fierce struggle in his own mind.

But how about the " common people "— the mass of those who were neither men of position nor Pharisees nor Zealots, who belonged to no particular sect or movement, but were mainly occupied in getting their bread? They had naturally taken delight in the new teacher who preached such a Gospel for the poor, and was so kind and unassuming, and had such wonderful power to heal and to help. But to them had come disillusionment, and of the large mass of those who showed a disposition at first to become disciples very few persevered. Jesus accounted for the situation in one of the most familiar of his parables—that of the Sower. There he describes the varieties of soil upon which the good seed of the word falls. Part of it is trodden hard by passers-by: that is the soul of those who hear but do not heed; part of it is rocky, where the soil is meagre: such is the soul of those who have no moral depth and in consequence no power of endurance; part of it is choked with thorns: such is the soul of men who allow material cares and desires so to preoccupy and possess their minds and wills as to "choke the word." This is an account of the situation which explains why, amidst the large following which gathered round Jesus at the beginning, so few came to be among the disciples he could depend upon.

For Jesus was no ordinary "reformer." The ordinary reformer sees clearly the abuses in contemporary societies which he passionately desires to get altered. But he feels that he must take men as he finds them, and make the best of the average material which comes to his hand; he is always prepared for compromises, and struggles simply to awaken and organize a movement strong enough to get his reforms carried. Now, Jesus was a reformer indeed; the Kingdom of God which he contemplated was an ideal kingdom of godliness, justice, peace and brotherhood, utterly unlike anything which he saw around him. And he was convinced that

THE GALILÆAN MINISTRY OF JESUS 79

its realization lay in the purpose of God—he was to found the new Israel in the heart of the old. But this would only be possible by bringing into being a new sort of human instrument which did not at present exist. This, as the story goes on, we shall find continually becoming more obvious. It is a fresh start which is demanded—a new humanity which has to be brought to the birth. Thus Jesus took a long view. He clearly anticipated, as we shall see, present failure—ignominy—disaster—death. But through all this dark night he saw the certain dawning of the new day. For that he must work. For his new structure he must find a rock-like foundation. He must educate a band to be the heart of the new Israel, whose devotion to God and his purposes shall be absolute, whose detachment from all other interests shall be complete, who shall be prepared for even the extreme sacrifice—ready for anything. We can understand little in the Gospels unless we understand in this way the method of Jesus, and how it led to his concentrating his attention upon the small company centring in the Twelve. This concentration belongs in the main to the second period of his ministry which we are not yet considering. But it explains the uncompromising, the extreme, character of his ethical teaching from the beginning. Really to listen to it and take it to heart—to have, as Jesus said, " ears to hear "—demanded an extraordinary degree of detachment. This will appear in more detail when we come to analyse " the Sermon on the Mount " as it appears in St. Matthew, or the more closely connected sermon which appears in St. Luke. But the " extreme " character of Jesus' moral claim becomes apparent to any one of us as soon as he begins to study any one of the Gospels. We can understand that those who first listened to him with any attention were compelled very soon to recognize that, as he himself said, he was asking more, not less, than the Pharisaic scribes asked of men. The innumerable rules, with which they hedged about the common actions of life, were indeed burdensome and annoying; but here in the new teaching of Jesus they found themselves confronted with a claim even more formidable than the most elaborate set of external rules— a claim that God should be so enthroned in the heart of man, as indisputably and only supreme, that his whole life should be moulded to his will and absorbed into the interests of his kingdom. The faith and trust that was asked of them was something much more than the acceptance of certain propositions about God

THE GALILÆAN MINISTRY OF JESUS

—it was entire self-surrender or self-committal to God. " Ye cannot," Jesus said, " serve God and Mammon." As the last analysis there will always be found one motive in life that is dominant. That motive must be God, and it must be all-absorbing. The " saving of your soul " or " self "—the realizing of your real being—requires that you should put God and His kingdom first and take the consequences. The kingdom indeed which is offered you is a " pearl of great price." It contains unimaginable riches. The life that you are called into is a glorious life. But if you are to receive much, you must be prepared to give much— even everything. If you are to buy the pearl of great price you must give all that you have to buy it. He that " saveth his life "—that is hugs himself tight as his own possession—shall lose himself and come to ruin; he only who abandons himself can find himself.

No one can read the Gospels and miss this note of absoluteness in the demand of Jesus upon the souls of men. It was not indeed that he despised or ignored the natural goodness which a man must be cynical indeed to refuse to see in the common actions of men. Jesus appreciated " a cup of cold water only " given in kindness. But he found this natural goodness of men—or the mixed quality of the average life around him—wholly inadequate for his purposes. " The Kingdom " could not be based on this sort of material, which is but a shifting sand. To describe what he wanted, he went back upon two requirements made on man in the name of God in the book of Deuteronomy (which appears, we may say, to have been his favourite book in the Jewish Bible). " Thou shalt love the Lord thy God with all thy heart and with all thy mind and with all thy soul and with all thy strength," and " Thou shalt love thy neighbour as thyself." The Greek word *agape* (translated " love " or " charity " in our English versions) is something fundamentally different from what we commonly think of as love. Indeed the Greek word for this " love " never occurs in the Greek of the New Testament. This love is a feeling or emotion, the instinctive, almost physical, emotion, which unites the mother to her child or friend to friend or man to woman. This, where it is aroused, may be a tremendous passion indeed, but it cannot be produced at will. But the word translated love in the New Testament expresses not an emotion at all. It is a fixed attitude of the will determining the direction of a man's life. To love God with all our heart,

THE GALILÆAN MINISTRY OF JESUS

soul, mind and strength, is deliberately to recognize in Him the ground and end of our being and to devote all the faculties of our nature to His service. This first and great commandment is thus an appeal to our wills, not to our feelings—not at least in the first instance, though ultimately the feeling may follow the concentration of the will. And the second commandment which is like unto it, "to love our neighbours as ourselves," has, again, no direct reference to feeling. "We must love the people we don't like." It is a deliberate acceptance of the fact that God has no favourites—that He created every man for a good end: and that the promotion of His kingdom means that we shall deliberately set ourselves to regard all men, and each man or woman, as God regards them—with impartial good will—and use our opportunities to serve His beneficent purpose for them, as genuinely and thoroughly as we should seek to serve our own true ends.

There are still two points which must be noted in connection with this all-embracing claim of Jesus upon those who would be his disciples—especially this all-embracing claim for devotion to God. This putting of God first meant a direct dealing with Him, as person with person : it meant a life of prayer. Jesus himself is always found seeking in prayer the strength and guidance to live and work, and he lays the greatest stress upon the efficacy of importunate asking. Indeed he uses the strangest metaphors to express the power of mere importunity, though as his teaching goes on he lays more stress on conforming our desires in prayer to the will of God. But while he lays this immense stress on praying, his teaching does not at all resemble that of the great mystics. There is little or nothing about absorption into God. The object for prayer appears to be rather to learn the will of God and have strength to carry out His purpose. Nothing is more noticeable than that he constantly insists that the devotion to God, to which he gives the first place, cannot express itself otherwise than in the service of man. It would appear that if we want to test ourselves as to whether we love God, the test is to be found in the genuineness of our love to our fellows, or in other words in the zeal with which we co-operate with God's great purpose of an equal good for all.

Once more it must be noticed that neither the life that Jesus lived nor the ideal of life which he inculcated was what is commonly called ascetic. Jesus did not live like John the

Baptist. Indeed it was made a matter of reproach against him that he did not. " John came eating no bread nor drinking wine, and ye say, he hath a devil. The son of man is come eating and drinking, and ye say, behold a gluttonous man and a wine-bibber, a friend of publicans and sinners." If we read the accounts, so frequent in St. Luke, of Jesus' attendance at " feasts," we see indeed how little he was occupied in the eating and drinking. His thoughts were on other things. Nor indeed can we read a page of the Gospels without seeing what thorough-going self-mastery and self-control his idea of life involved. If by asceticism is meant self-discipline, Jesus' ideal of life was thoroughly ascetic. But it is plain that what he was preparing was a band of men who would live in the world, mingling as he mingled in the common life of men, its labours, its joys, its sorrows—only bent on transforming this common life into something infinitely rich and rare. His claim upon his disciples was heroic rather than ascetic.

This general account of the character and tone of Jesus' ethical claim and teaching has made it very obvious how it came about that the first popularity of his preaching passed away. Not only did the leaders of society

86   JESUS OF NAZARETH

hate him, but the common people who had "heard him gladly" found his claim too much for them. Even in his own family, apart from his mother, he found no support—"Neither did his brethren believe in him."[1] So we understand how it was that he came to concentrate all his attention on the training of the Twelve in view of the great future for which he was preparing. It becomes more and more obvious that Jesus was a Founder: he was preparing an instrument which should fulfil his purpose after he was gone.

This concentration is what characterizes the second period of his ministry. The transition from the one to the other may be found in three events, or groups of events, which hold a central place in the Gospels.

First of these pivots we reckon the Mission of the Twelve, when they were sent out two by two as heralds of the kingdom. They were to go out totally resourceless—without money or food or change of raiment—with nothing but a staff. They were to go without the support of his presence, but Jesus is represented as clothing them with something of his own power

---

[1] The "brethren" were probably older than Jesus—strictly half-brethren, or sons of Joseph by a former wife.

THE GALILÆAN MINISTRY OF JESUS 87

over spirits of evil and bodily diseases; and they were to go in his name from village to village to announce the kingdom, claiming support and a respectful hearing as messengers of God; and if they were not received in any place they were to "shake off the dust of their feet" for a testimony of judgement against the men of that place. They came back exhilarated by the power they had experienced and apparently the welcome they had received. Jesus took them away to rest awhile in a desert place, seemingly at the north of the lake near Bethsaida, but an immense crowd, perhaps stimulated by the mission, followed them and broke in upon them; and the compassion of Jesus brought him among them to "teach them many things." Then, resourceless as they were, after three days, he fed them—five thousand men, without counting women and children—with the few barley loaves and fishes which was all the provision which the disciples had brought with them. "And they did all eat and were filled," and they took up basketfuls of the broken pieces.

The second pivot is the escape of Jesus from Galilee and the ending of his mission there.

After the feeding of the Five Thousand the crowd would have come by force and made him a king: but Jesus evaded this misdirected enthusiasm, and it would seem to be at this point in the story that he left Galilee and went a long tour extending to the neighbourhood of Tyre and Sidon, quite outside " the Holy Land " northward, and passing through Philip's territory to the district of Decapolis. The motive of this appears to have been threefold: first to escape the momentary enthusiasm which he was convinced was not, and would not become, the kind of faith he needed; secondly, because he desired to have the Twelve with him by themselves, and this long journey gave him the opportunity (only Matthew expressly tells us that he took the Twelve with him, but it can hardly be doubted); thirdly, because the news had come to him that Herod Antipas had at last allowed Herodias to have her way and had murdered John the Baptist in the fortress of Machærus. Jesus may well have felt that Herod would seek his life also. But " his time was not yet come ": nor was he to be prevented from making the visit to Jerusalem. So he left the territory of Herod. Exact chronology or geography is not the strong point of either Mark's or Luke's narrative and we cannot be sure that he ever returned to it.

The third point which connects the two

stages of the ministry of Jesus is the solemn confession of his Messiahship by Peter, the leader of the Apostles. It occurred in a spot calculated to damp the enthusiasm of any Israelite—the neighbourhood of Cæsarea Philippi. The name of the city and the associations of the district spoke of the dominance of Rome and Greece, and it was there that Jesus tested the Twelve by a direct question about himself, "Who do men say that I am?" The answer was that all were agreed that he was someone with a divine commission—perhaps the Elijah who was to herald the coming of the Christ, or one of the prophets, or John the Baptist again. But Jesus is not satisfied with hearing what others think of him. He presses them more closely. "But who do ye say that I am?" He expects a more definite conviction in those who have been so much closer to him. And Peter, the bold leader and spokesman of the Twelve, answered him, "Thou art the Christ." The solemn benediction pronounced on him by Jesus—"Blessed art thou, Simon, son of John . . . and I say unto thee that thou art Peter (Rock-man) and on this rock I will build my church (my new Israel)"—occurs only in St. Matthew, but it precisely fits into the critical situation. Jesus now at last can feel that amidst the vague opinions, which were so much shifting sand, he has found something rock-like on which to build. Henceforth it was an open secret between Jesus and the Twelve that he was the promised Messiah. But they were bidden to keep it strictly secret from all but their own circle. The reason for this secrecy became at once obvious. It was because the current ideas of the Christ were so far from the truth, and not even the Twelve, it appeared, were capable of accepting the truth as Jesus conceived it. At once Jesus told them that knowing himself to be the Christ he knew that his destiny was that announced by the Second Isaiah for the Servant of Jehovah. He must suffer many things and be rejected and be killed—only so could he come into his heritage. Peter protested with a friendly gesture —"This be far from thee, Lord." But this deprecation of suffering sounds in Jesus' ears as the very voice of Satan. "Get thee behind me, Satan!" he cries to the Peter whom he had just so richly blessed. But at this point of connection between the two periods of the ministry we must leave the story for a while to examine a little more closely some points in the teaching of Jesus.

CHAPTER III

THE TEACHING OF JESUS

IN sketching the Galilæan ministry of Jesus it has been necessary to give some general idea of the content of his teaching. As has already appeared it was almost wholly ethical—a bringing into vivid light of the character of the Kingdom of God and of its citizens. A certain doctrine of God as "the Father" dominated all he said, and it was given out in a tone of absolute assurance, as by one who knew beyond possibility of mistake. Others ideas or doctrines which would be called theological are no doubt implied, and sometimes indeed affirmed, but what alone was constant and unmistakable in the Galilæan preaching was that Jesus was labouring to bring those who had ears to hear to the understanding of a way of life, which was to be the way of the New Israel. Again, this ethical teaching of Jesus was not expounded as a philosopher or legislator might expound a system. It was given by way of proverbs or aphorisms—sometimes highly paradoxical aphorisms—and parables. This method of Jesus demands first of all some detailed notice.

1. *The Method of Jesus*

As it has recently been interpreted very fully by the late Dr. Burney in *The Poetry of Our Lord*, the method of Jesus' teaching was largely the method of Hebrew poetry—the method of " parallelism," which has long been familiar to students of the Psalms and prophecies of the Old Testament, and which was still used by some of the Rabbis, such as Hillel.

According to this method the idea to be conveyed is expressed in rhythmical couplets or triplets or four-line stanzas—occasionally with the help of rhyme; and the " parallelism " may be of different kinds. Thus it may be " synonymous "—each line expressing the same idea in different forms, as in:

> " He that is not with me is against me
> (And) he that gathereth not with me scattereth."
> " This thy brother was dead and is alive again,
> He was lost and is found."

Or it may be " antithetic " as in

> " He that findeth his life shall lose it ;
> He that loseth his life for my sake shall find it."

THE TEACHING OF JESUS   93

Or it may be "synthetic" where the second line interprets the first :

" And call no man your father upon earth ;
For one is your Father, which is in heaven."

Or it may be "step parallelism" where the second line repeats and adds something to the first :

" He that receiveth you, receiveth me
And he that receiveth me, receiveth him that sent me."

All these forms are familiar in the Old Testament and in the Gospels. Burney thus expresses his conclusion, " We find this form of parallelism characterizes Our Lord's teaching in all the Gospel-sources. . . . This is conclusive evidence that Our Lord did so frame his teaching ; and it is obvious that a maxim cast in antithetic parallelism would fix itself in men's minds more readily and surely than if it were framed in any other form. . . . In this and in similar forms of antithesis we may surely believe that we possess our Lord's *ipsissima verba* more nearly than in any sentence otherwise expressed." Burney is speaking of one particular kind of parallelism : but what he says is true, more or less, of all of them. It is a mode of expression which renders even the exact words of a teacher easily rememberable. And we should note that, as is generally the case among a people who have hardly any books, the memory of the Jews was a highly cultivated faculty. The object of their schools was to secure the accurate recollection and repetition of the teacher's phrases.

It becomes also evident on reflection that this method of parallelism leaves little room for modification or fullness of statements, but is built upon what we may call proverbs. Now, proverbs are pregnant maxims, easily remembered and general in form, but so little covering the whole ground of experience as often to be on the face of them contradictory, as when we say " Penny wise, pound foolish," and then, again, " Take care of the pence and the pounds will take care of themselves " ; or when Jesus said, " He that is not with me is against me," and on another occasion, " He that is not against you is for you." Each proposition is intelligible and we can appreciate its truth. But each is pointed at a particular class of cases without any care taken to correlate one with the other. Proverbs, then, are principles stated in extremes, without modification, often requiring to be balanced by their seeming contraries.

We cannot pursue this rather fascinating subject, but, if we read the teaching of Jesus

THE TEACHING OF JESUS 95

in any of the Gospels, we see how much of it has the character just described, and needs to be interpreted with this in mind. It is especially necessary for a rather prosaic people like ourselves to observe this. When Jesus says, "If thy right eye causeth thee to stumble, pluck it out and cast it from thee," or "If any man would go to law with thee and take away thy coat, let him have thy cloke also," or "There are eunuchs which have made themselves eunuchs for the kingdom of heaven's sake," he is in each case giving an extremely important piece of direction or guidance for life: but he puts it proverbially in an extreme form which does not admit of being reduced to a prosaic general statement of man's duty. We need to get at the principle behind the proverb—at the same time not forgetting that the sharp-pointed paradoxical form of the instruction is meant to stimulate us, and to warn us that the conduct required of us in such and such cases will be extreme and difficult conduct.

Another caution is needed in view of Jewish habits of speech. There are a great number of sentences in the Bible built upon the framework "not . . . but": e.g. "Labour *not* for the meat that perisheth, *but* for that which endureth unto life eternal." Two hundred examples have been counted in the Gospels alone. Some of these phrases mean exactly what is said, that is, the first alternative is literally excluded. But more often it is intended only to depreciate the first by comparison with the second, as in the case quoted above, where Jesus certainly did not mean to condemn what elsewhere he approves—honest work for an honest living—but only intended to fix our attention on a more important kind of labour. Similarly the Bible sometimes contrasts " loving " one and " hating " another, where we should speak more prosaically of preferring one to the other.

The second marked characteristic of Jesus' teaching was his use of parables. The parables of Jesus, as they appear in the world's literature, are masterpieces : we are not surprised to find that the disciples who first heard them did not, when they came to be teachers, attempt to imitate them : and again they are easily rememberable—we may almost say unforgettable. Under the vague head of parables, we comprise different sorts of utterances. There are stories with a moral, like Dives and Lazarus, or the Rich Fool, where there is no " hidden meaning " ; there are imaginary descriptions of the ways of God, like the scene of the Last Judgement,

THE TEACHING OF JESUS 97

where the earthly analogies are barely alluded to ; and there are parables proper, where some familiar process of nature or of man is described at length, and we are bidden to think what it means and to understand that it supplies an analogy for the spiritual kingdom and the dealings of God with us. These parables proper appear to be based upon a deep principle—that any " law of nature," or anything fundamentally characteristic of human conduct (even in bad men), is a revelation of the divine. God and his ways are to be looked for and discovered in nature and in anything fundamentally human. Sometimes Jesus explained his parables to his disciples, who were a very unimaginative group. " Are ye," he complained, " yet so without understanding ? " But he also came to use parables without explanations as a test of moral seriousness. Every one would listen with pleasure to the story : every one no doubt would recognize that Jesus meant something by it, more than appeared on the surface of the story : but only a few would " have ears to hear," that is, would take the trouble to understand what exactly he meant and pay heed to it, when they had understood it. Thus a parable acted as a judgement.

It should be added that just as Homer and

later poets, in their similitudes, elaborate the picture, sometimes beyond the requirements of its application, so it is in the parables of Jesus. The point of each parable is one only. Thus though the story of the prodigal son, in the parable we call by that name, and of his ready welcome by his father, is necessary to give the parable its background, we do not really get to the point till we get to the conduct of the elder brother. This parable, we must remember, was addressed to the Pharisees, who had complained of Jesus receiving sinners and eating with them. When a parable, as we find it in the Gospels, has two points quite distinct, like the parable of the Pounds (in Luke xix. 11), we suspect that we have a fusion of originally distinct parables.

Quite apart from the lessons of the parables, no one who studies them, and considers the variety of aspects of nature and human character and occupations which appears in them, can fail to appreciate the richness and accuracy of the faculty of observation in the Son of Man.

Of course, Jesus does not always speak in parables or proverbs. We have also denunciations, observations and instructions given often in response to some urgent question, though very seldom giving " the plain answer to the

THE TEACHING OF JESUS 99

plain question." But even so in all Jesus' teaching the parabolic and the proverbial methods are near at hand.

2. The "Sermon on the Mount"

For a prolonged example of the teaching of Jesus we will take the Sermon on the Mount, in which, beyond doubt, Matthew has collected into one sermon utterances delivered on various occasions. Many of these utterances are found in Luke distributed in different parts of his narrative; but some—most memorable and undoubtedly authentic—occur only in Matthew's version, and we will take that version as a whole for our first study. Dr. Burney argues for the superiority of Matthew's reports of Jesus' teaching over those given in Mark or Luke, where they differ, at many points—for example, he prefers on grounds of rhythm Matthew's longer versions of the Lord's Prayer and of the Beatitudes to those of Luke. But surely we should imagine that Jesus often repeated the same lesson in different forms on different occasions, and different versions may be both authentic memories.

However, without further preface, we will pass to the Sermon—deepest and most arresting of all sermons—as given in Matt. v.–vii. It is definitely *addressed to* the inner circle, the disciples, but *overheard by* the larger crowd, representing the world. It begins with the Beatitudes—I suppose we may say the most pregnant and powerful group of aphorisms in the whole of human literature. They describe the character of citizens of the Kingdom in phrases which, first of all, put the true idea of blessedness into startling contradiction to the accepted ideas of the world. " Blessed are the poor (or ' ye poor ')—blessed are the mourners—blessed are the meek " ! These startling sayings have a personal application. The little group around Jesus consisted of men undoubtedly poor—destined undoubtedly to have much reason for tears—and to be very much wronged. But they are the really well-off ! Jesus goes on to describe the character by its positive notes—the passion for righteousness—the overmastering motive of pity—the singleness of aim (that is the meaning of " purity of heart ")—the love of peace. Then he ends by announcing the destiny of such a character in such a world as that of our present experience—persecution and malignant misrepresentation—to be met by its victims with an unfeigned delight that they are admitted to share the destiny of the saints of old (v. 1-12).

THE TEACHING OF JESUS 101

The central point in the Master's plan of campaign is next made plain. He is not propounding an ideal which the world will welcome. The disciples will be few among many. He is creating a spiritual aristocracy consisting of those who are content to give all for all. They are to be in the world as the salt which purifies by its distinctive savour: as a light which shines in a dark place: as a city set on a hill. The whole secret of Jesus is here (v. 13-16).

Then he defines his relation to the moral Law of the old Covenant. It was of God and every detail of it has to be so far obeyed. But it was all imperfect and demands fulfilment. The more spiritual law which Jesus propounds authoritatively is harder, not easier, than the old law of external actions, which the scribes and Pharisees had elaborated in infinite detail. So he proceeds to deal with the sixth commandment (as we call it)—" Thou shalt do no murder " —by pressing it back from the outward act of murder to the first inwardly allowed feeling, or hasty utterance, of hatred or contempt. Such hatred or scorn is now to be ranked as the equivalent of murder, and each grade of sin is to find its appropriate judgement. Thus the first conscious beginnings of enmity must be hastily dealt with and obliterated, or the judgement will become inevitable (v. 21–6).

Then Jesus deals with the seventh commandment—" Thou shalt not commit adultery." Henceforth it must be understood that the will to sin is the sin itself. It is the inner will that has to be made secure. Deliberately a man should prefer security at the centre to freedom at the circumference of life. Even self-mutilation is better than total and final ruin. Incidentally here marriage is pronounced indissoluble and divorce abolished. The meaning of the apparent exception in St. Matthew—" Save for the cause of fornication"—remains uncertain. But scholars are almost all agreed that the law without exception, as given in St. Paul and St. Mark and St. Luke, is the law as Jesus pronounced it (v. 27–32).

The third commandment—against false swearing—is next dealt with. The use of oaths under any circumstances, i.e. the invoking of God on special occasions, has its origin in evil. All speech must be lifted to the level of the oath by God, for all speech is in fact uttered in God's presence and all power is ultimately His (v. 33–7).

Another point appears: the law of exact retaliation (an ancient restriction on the freedom

THE TEACHING OF JESUS 103

of revenge) is to have its place taken by an utter readiness to submit even to grossest injustice. (It does not, however, follow that when the will of any outraged individual has been disciplined to perfect meekness, social duty may not require judicial action. Jesus himself claimed justice, and was believed from the first to have enjoined judicial action within the community of the brethren: Matt. xviii. 15-17.) Again, all limits upon the requirement of charity are removed. Enemies and persecutors are brought under its scope. The Father loves all men of all sorts; and the brethren, those who have been taken into the family of the Father, must acquiesce in nothing short of His all-embracing charity. (One may perhaps wish that the word "charity" had been retained everywhere in the New Testament in place of the word "love." For as has been explained, love in all languages expresses a feeling or an emotion, and the Greek word *Agape*, now in the Revised Version everywhere translated *love*, describes not an emotion at all, but a deliberate disposition of the will. The Greek word "eros," which describes the emotion or passion of love, never occurs in the New Testament.)

There follows an instruction on the purging of the motive of religious activities from all regard to man's approval, under the three heads of almsgiving (the merit of which ranked highest among the Jews), fasting, and prayer. Characteristically it is expressed in extreme forms such as, verbally interpreted, would exclude not only the motive of seeking human applause, but the doing of the action at all when under observation. Incidentally, true prayer is distinguished from " heathen " praying, in that he who prays truly does not imagine that God can be affected by babblings because they are long-continued, or can need to be informed about our wants. Then the distinctive character of true prayer is shown by an example. The " Lord's Prayer " is, we may say, the pattern of all prayer " in Christ's name "—

"Our Father, which art in heaven : hallowed be thy name :

Thy Kingdom come : thy will be done :

As in heaven, so on earth.

Give us to-day our bread for the coming day :

And forgive us our debts, as we too have forgiven our debtors :

And lead us not into temptation, but deliver us from the evil one."

The order of the clauses here given suggests the whole philosophy not only of prayer but of life. The true function of man on earth is to correspond with the gracious purpose of God, and allow His kingdom to come into being on earth, even as in the heavenly world it is already realized. So we are to pray, placing ourselves solemnly in the presence of the common Father, that, as in heaven so on earth, His name may be hallowed, His kingdom may come and His will may be done. All that the individual has need to ask for himself is to be subordinated to that large purpose, i.e. the supply of his needs, the forgiveness of his sins, his defence against evil. It may be said that any child can understand the Lord's Prayer: but to pray it with honest and full purpose of heart requires both the faith of a child and the courage of a hero.

Jesus further explains how the motive of human life is to be purged and simplified. God and His will is to be put in sole and sovereign control. All then will follow in due course. The supreme aim cannot be too exclusively pursued. Our wills are ours to make them God's. No rival object of devotion is to be admitted. Granted this, God will provide for a man as he does for the birds and the flowers. What folly is anxiety! What can it accomplish? Every day we should face the requirements of the day without fear for the future, simply trusting God (chap. vi.)

The "sermon" as given by Matthew then takes up again the topic of "charity." (Probably the version of the sermon in Luke vi. 20-49 gives the scope of the original instruction—the other topics in Matthew's sermon belonging to other occasions.) Abstinence from judging others, considering what we are ourselves, is insisted upon without the mention of any qualification. One qualification, however, is at once suggested. We are to discriminate in our estimate of men, and to offer our real treasures to those only who can appreciate them (vii. 1-6). Then a series of vigorous metaphors removes all idea that our attitude towards God is to be a merely passive and submissive attitude. God will not be found to act on our behalf except in correspondence with our vigorous demand and importunate asking. The secret of effective prayer however, we have already been taught, is the conformity of our wills to God's. That means freedom from any preference of ourselves over others, or of our own convenience over theirs. So the paragraph ends on the note of unselfishness as the summary requirement (vii. 7-12).

Finally it is emphasized that the disciple of

THE TEACHING OF JESUS 107

Jesus must wholly refuse to consider majorities in directing the way of his life. The majority is always going wrong. The real guidance is to be found no doubt in the teaching of the Spirit of God by His prophets; but there are false prophets as well as true. Prophets are to be tested by their moral conduct, and so also disciples of Jesus. Jesus is now speaking to men in the name of God. But one day he will come upon them in judgement. It will then be of no avail to have listened to him and taken pleasure in his words and re-echoed them: even marvellous powers of control over evil spirits, exercised in his name, will be of no avail: nothing will avail in the great hour of trial except a life based firmly and wholly on his word (vii. 13–27).

No one can mistake the meaning of this discourse, which seems to gather into one the teaching of Jesus. It means that his purpose was indeed revolutionary. The kingdom he came to inaugurate was to be a life of fellowship, human and divine, so thorough in its whole conception that, for those who were satisfied with existing societies, it would seem to turn human relationships upside down, and to be quite impracticable. But Jesus was in the world for no other purpose than to bring into existence a new Israel, consisting of those who by the courage of faith should find it practicable and make it real. Now we must turn to his conception of the Messiah in whom the New Israel was to find its centre.

3. *The Idea of the Messiah*

One dominant aim of the old prophets of Israel was to proclaim the certainty that, although God was content age after age to allow the rebellious wills of men to usurp dominion in the world, and to seem to have it all their own way, yet He was at last to come into His own in His whole creation, and establish in undisputed sovereignty His justice and mercy and truth. Modern writers have made a mistake, however, in saying that the " kingdom of God," which the prophets foresaw, meant nothing else than God's reign or sovereignty. It always was a concrete idea in their minds. What they foresaw was the sovereignty of God realized in Israel and centring in Jerusalem. This of course involved the putting down and annihilating of all hostile powers and institutions. " The day of the Lord shall be upon all that is proud and haughty and it shall be brought low." In the noblest prophetic utterances the

THE TEACHING OF JESUS 109

consummate victory over all hostile forces was to be only the prelude to the union of all nations in the gracious fellowship of Israel. Egypt and Babylon, Philistia and Tyre were to learn to call Jerusalem their mother. But in many passages of the prophetic writings a lower patriotism prevails, and it suffices to foresee the utter destruction of the enemy. " Thou shalt bruise them with a rod of iron and break them in pieces like a potter's vessel." In the latter period of Israel's history—as in the Pharisaic *Psalms of Solomon* (about 50 B.C.)—they had become content with that lower vision. All that is contemplated is the destruction of the " godless peoples ". and the purging and glorifying of Israel.

Two further points must be noted in this forecast of the divine kingdom—first that the prophets have no map of the future in their minds. They constantly foresee the advent of the day of God in the immediate future. But constant failures to see what they had expected never damped the assurance that, as surely as God is God, He must come into His own at last.

Secondly, under the succession of the kings of the family of David in Judah, the future instrument of divine victory, and administrator of divine righteousness, is foreseen as an anointed king of David's house. At the centre of the Kingdom is the King. This is the Messianic vision which possessed the mind of Israel when Jesus' ministry began: and the idea of the king had lent itself, of course, only too readily to militarist ideals. But there was another idea which appears in the later Jewish apocalypses, of which we have got one of the best specimens in the Second Book of Esdras in our "Apocrypha." These apocalypses are forecasts of the future, put into the mouths of primeval or ancient heroes—such as Adam, Noah, Enoch, David, Baruch, Ezra. They belong to the centuries immediately before and after the coming of Jesus. They were soon frowned upon by the Jewish rabbis—except the Book of Daniel; and, while they were popular in early Christian times, the Christian Church also finally rejected them, and most of them have only recently been recovered in translations, more or less interpolated by Christian scribes. A great deal of attention has been paid to them by modern scholars, and an exaggerated importance has often been attached to them. One frequent characteristic of them is that in their forecast of the future, instead of the renewal of this earth, with Jerusalem as its centre, which is the forecast of the prophets, they anticipate the utter passing away of the present material heaven and earth and the establishment of a wholly new world: and in the *Similitudes of the Book of Enoch*, instead of the earth-born Christ, the son of David, we have introduced to us, as the divinely commissioned agent and bringer-in of the new world, a heavenly being, not really a man, but like to a man, and called " that Son of Man." This last-named book was current perhaps a century before the birth of Jesus. Its imagery is based upon the vision in the Book of Daniel, where the world powers are represented by " four great beasts " and Israel—" the people of the saints of the most high," which is to overcome them and take their place—is represented by " one like to a son of man, whose kingdom is to be an everlasting kingdom, and all dominions shall serve and obey him." But in Enoch the " one like to a son of man " has become—not Israel, but an individual—a heavenly being who is substituted for the traditional human-born Messiah of the House of David.

Now, as has been said already, two things are certain: first, that it was the traditional figure of the human Son of David, as the future

Messiah, which occupied the imagination of Israel when Jesus came; secondly, that when he called himself "the son of man," it was a non-committal title, which was not understood by the people as a claim on his part to be Messiah, and was not so intended. Even when Jesus, at the end of his life, spoke about the Son of Man revealed in glory, his language does not need anything to interpret it but Daniel's vision, except on one point—that the "one like to a son of man" in that vision had come to mean in Jesus' mind an individual and not the holy nation, just as in the Book of Enoch, and that individual himself.

This must suffice as background for the understanding of the novel interpretation which Jesus finally gave to the idea of the Messiah or Christ.

He accepted the ascription to himself of the old traditional prophetic idea of the Christ King, the Son of David; but, as it were, reluctantly, because he felt its militarist associations and its inadequacy. He accepted also and used at last the conception of the Son of Man coming in glory. But to both these conceptions he gave a wholly new meaning by interpreting "the Son of Man" in terms of the picture which the later Isaiah had drawn of the Suffering

THE TEACHING OF JESUS 113

Servant of Jehovah who was to redeem Israel. That figure also had originally meant not an individual but the people Israel, or rather " the faithful remnant " of that people, as it was to return purged and sanctified from Babylon. But Jesus interpreted it of an individual, of himself. And indeed that most familiar chapter of Isaiah (liii.), which describes the despised sufferer and martyr, unjustly condemned and put to death, who makes his life an offering for the sins of his people and through death becomes their prevailing intercessor, presents to us irresistibly, as we read it, the idea of an individual. Beyond all reasonable question Jesus identified this figure with himself. After Peter's confession of his Messiahship, it becomes the central point of his teaching, within the inner circle of the Twelve, that, here and nowhere else are they to find the true picture of the Messiah. This was wholly to rob the traditional idea of the Son of David of all its militarist and worldly associations. It was to introduce, as the central thought of the New Israel, the idea of redemption, not by force, but by humiliation and sacrifice. It was this that in its extreme form was represented by the sadly familiar symbol of the Cross. Only at the climax is this sacrificial death to pass into glory, and the rejected and crucified Son of Man is to be found exalted to sovereign lordship—" at the right hand " of God. In a word, Jesus transformed both the traditional idea of the Christ-King and the apocalyptic idea of the glorified form from heaven, by merging them both in Isaiah's picture of the suffering Redeemer. It was this " doctrine of the cross " which he pressed down upon the minds of the reluctant disciples, even as we shall see at the cost of causing their faith for the time to fail.

4. *The Coming of the Kingdom*

In such a little book as this it is not possible to discuss controversial questions with any fullness. But it is impossible to pass over altogether in silence the recent revival—especially under the influence of Albert Schweitzer—of the idea of Jesus as a prophet wholly absorbed in the apocalyptic idea of the Christ as the glorified " Son of Man " who was to come from heaven to judge this world and to bring in the world to come. According to this view, then, Jesus did not believe himself to *be* the Christ while he was walking the earth ; but only to be destined to be the Christ when he should have been rapt to heaven and should return in glory. This, we are told, he at first anticipated would

THE TEACHING OF JESUS 115

come about immediately, without any interposition of death. Afterwards he was convinced that he must (so to speak) force the issue by giving his life in sacrifice at Jerusalem. Then God would vindicate him at once, and he would be sent from heaven as the Christ, to judge and to destroy the old world and bring in the new. Jesus then, wholly possessed by this idea, never dreamed of preparing for a future upon earth by the foundation of a Church of his disciples. He can hardly be described rightly as an ethical teacher at all. His conception of the relation of men to God and to their fellow men does indeed involve an absolute ethic which is of everlasting value; but the practical ethic which Jesus taught was only an " ethic of the interval," the very brief interval of months before his coming as the Christ. And this ethic was simply the ethic of world-renunciation. All that he aimed at was to instruct the loyal few who adhered to him to cut themselves loose from all attachment to the world, that they might be ready for the miraculous event from heaven.

In recent days we have had this visionary fanatic presented to us as the true picture of Jesus, as well as its direct opposite, the " Liberal Protestant " Christ, who is little more than an ethical prophet with wonderful gifts as a healer, all the " apocalyptic " elements in the picture being reduced to a minimum or even wholly omitted, and attributed to the Jewish fanaticism of the first disciples. Again, we have had a third representation of Jesus which depicts him as starting indeed with the purest ethical intentions, but gradually succumbing to the lower influences and fanatical enthusiasms around him. But it is surely uncritical wilfulness in dealing with our documents—which after all, we shall find, are on a high level of trustworthiness—to take one part of the evidence and ignore the rest. No one can deny that in our Gospels, and certainly in those of Mark and Luke, you have got the picture of an ethical master, preparing the faithful few to be the new Israel, to proclaim the good tidings to the world and exhibit to the world a new pattern of human life. No one, on the other hand, can deny that the apocalyptic expectation is also attributed to Jesus. But are the two ideas at all incompatible ? As to the third representation of Jesus which we referred to, there are no grounds to be found in the evidence for any profound change of plan or deterioration of character or of ideal in Jesus during his ministry. No great teacher was ever less subject to influences from without.

THE TEACHING OF JESUS 117

We will proceed then to build our representation of Jesus' teaching about the coming of the kingdom on the evidence as a whole—making the reasonable claim that, if an intelligible representation can so be fashioned, it is better " criticism " to accept it, than to take refuge in any representation of him which can only justify itself by ignoring large parts of the evidence, which have quite as strong a claim to acceptance as that portion which is adopted.

Jesus, then, came preaching the good tidings of the kingdom, which, it appeared, had now actually come upon men in his coming, and which was evidenced in his power over diseases and over the spirits of evil. His message was to Israel only, as God's chosen people : as it was in Israel first of all that the promised kingdom was to be realized. Like John the Baptist, his forerunner, he made it clear that Israel as it stood needed a fundamental change of mind before it could welcome the kingdom. Very soon, however, it appeared that there were very few in Israel who would respond to the tremendous demand he made upon men. For various causes class after class showed itself obdurate in refusal of him. Then Jesus acted like the old prophets under similar circumstances. He turned from the mass of the people to the "faithful remnant," and he proceeded to fashion out of them a new Israel fit for their high destiny. " Fear not, little flock," he said to them, "it is my Father's good pleasure to give you the kingdom."

The Sermon on the Mount may be described as the Law of the Kingdom or of the reformed Israel; and the first step in its reorganization was taken by the choice of the Twelve as "apostles," who are to be found at last as the "judges" of its "twelve tribes." In parables which represent Israel as the vineyard or the household of God, it is made evident that, the old keepers of the Vineyard or stewards of the Household having proved faithless, it is to be handed over to new management. More and more clearly it appears that Jesus is looking beyond his death and preparing the Twelve to carry on his work after he has gone. Also it appears that they are to expect to find themselves rejected and persecuted even as Jesus himself, for a period, but not for ever. For " the Day of the Son of Man " will come at last. When in fact we see the first Christian Church beginning its career in the Acts, it is as an organized body under the Apostles, with a teaching of its own, and an equipment of simple rites of spiritual fellowship which it claimed

THE TEACHING OF JESUS 119

to have received from its Master. They are threatened with persecution and are quite ready for it. But they are eagerly expecting the *immediate* return of their Master. It is recorded however that on two occasions the disciples had questioned him when that would be, and on the first occasion he had replied that even he himself had no map of the future spread before his eyes—he did not know "the day and the hour"; and on the second occasion, under quite different circumstances, he had told them that it was not for them to know times and seasons which the Father had reserved in his own control. All that they had to do was to bear their witness, in the power of the Spirit of God, which they were to expect to be immediately given them from on high, for a period that was left quite indefinite. Unless we are to discard a large half of our evidence about Jesus we must admit that the first stage in the realization of the kingdom, as Jesus saw it, lay in the instruction, rudimentary organization, and equipment of the New Israel, the Church of the Messiah. If the Church was not to be in the full sense the kingdom, it was at least to be its vestibule, and its representative on earth. Thus if Jesus, standing among his disciples, speaks of some among them who, before they die, shall have " seen the kingdom " or " seen it come with power," and if, standing before Caiaphas, he declares that " henceforth " or " from this moment " they shall see realized Daniel's vision of the Son of Man in divine power, his words are satisfied by the events which followed his death and gave the Church that sense of glory and power reflected from Christ, which was the secret of its surprising success, and which inspired in their adversaries a kind of terror.

But there was another stage in the manifestation of the kingdom which Jesus accepted from the prophets of Israel—that is, the judgement upon the hostile world-power. Any reader of the Old Testament is familiar with the oracles of judgement upon Assyria, upon Babylon, upon Tyre, upon Edom. When Jesus first announced himself in the synagogue at Nazareth as sent to fulfil the promise of the kingdom, he omitted (as we noted) the last clause of the announcement which he took from Isaiah—" the day of vengeance of our God." For the present it was the time of open opportunity and nothing else. But the opportunity was refused : the offer was rejected. There must follow therefore inevitable judgement—not now on some pagan empire, but on apostate Israel. The Gospels represent

THE TEACHING OF JESUS 121

Jesus as recognizing with passionate grief, and announcing explicitly in private to his disciples, that the final sentence of judgement on Jerusalem and on its temple had gone forth. " The days of vengeance " must now be expected, and " this generation shall not pass away till all things are accomplished." This sentence on Jerusalem was in fact executed within the generation (forty years) after his death. But obviously this sort of " day of judgement " may be repeated time after time on many a corrupted civilization and institution. There are many " days of the Son of Man " in this sense.

But again, in the manner of the ancient prophets, and using their very words, Jesus threw this judgement on Jerusalem upon the background of a great world-cataclysm. These old prophets, and Jesus himself, are obviously using metaphorical language. The rending heavens—the failing sun and moon—the falling stars—the trumpet sound—the descending form of majesty—the great white throne—the gathering nations—the open book—the sentence of judgement—these are metaphors; but they are metaphors expressive of a great idea—that the manifest vindication of God against all hostile and rebel wills is at last to be a fact: that, as surely as God is God, He is at the climax of this world's history to come into His own in His whole universe. This is, in the full and final sense, the coming of the kingdom of God. In the apocalyptic language of Jesus it appears, as we have said, as the background of the judgement on Jerusalem. In one of the versions (Matthew's) it is made its " immediate " sequel. In Luke's version this is not so. There can be no doubt that we cannot in this matter decide between the Gospels as to what exactly Jesus said. But we can rely upon it that there was a certain judgement (on Jerusalem) which he did pronounce to be speedily imminent, and some other kind of judgement or final " day of the Lord," of which he declared that he himself did not know the date, or again that it was not for the disciples to know it, for it was a reserved secret in the breast of God.

The following propositions, then, we shall see, if we try to judge the evidence impartially, to be fairly certain.

The whole substance of the teaching of Jesus was "the Gospel of the Kingdom " as having now come upon men in his person.

When his message was not received by the mass of the nation, he instructs and organizes the faithful remnant—the disciples—to be the new Israel of the Messiah under the Twelve.

THE TEACHING OF JESUS 123

In them the kingdom of God is to go out into the world in spiritual power, even though still weak in secular resources and persecuted even to death.

He announces another speedy sign of the kingdom in the judgement on apostate Jerusalem speedily to be executed.

Finally he proclaims an end or climax to this whole world-order, upon which a new world-order shall supervene, in which God shall be all in all; but this final manifestation of judgement and justice he refused altogether to date.

Any careful student of the Gospels will feel that on this matter of the Kingdom there is some considerable confusion in the Gospels and some considerable difference in tone—for instance as between St. Matthew and St. Luke, or still more between St. Matthew and St. John. St. Luke, and much more St. John, appear to be deliberately correcting what they believed to be a mistaken impression of the Master's teaching: but on the main lines of it we can feel secure. If the account of it which has been given here is fairly true, we can now appreciate in its true character the " other-worldliness " of Jesus.

5. The "Other-worldliness" of Jesus

There can be no question that Jesus refused altogether to regard this world as a complete thing. He has always in view another " supernatural " world which is equally real, which is called " heaven," which is one day to absorb and transform this world. Meanwhile this world considered by itself is a place of probation or preparation for the world to come, both a " vale of soul-making " and a place of kingdom-building. Certainly Jesus affirms that each individual personality subsists beyond death and reaps there as he has sown here. Each has the making of his own soul or self—the awful capacity to save or to destroy himself.

When he was questioned by the Sadducees, who denied the resurrection of the dead, he replied plainly and decisively that in their conflict with the Pharisees on this matter they were in error : " Ye do err, not knowing the Scripture, neither the power of God." But though Jesus thus decisively affirmed the idea, already part of the common creed of the Jews, of resurrection and retribution in the world beyond, and though he used language implying an intermediate state of rest or punishment, and an ultimate heaven and hell, he never made the world to come a subject of detailed instruction. He plainly did intend his disciples to calculate life on the eternal scale and on the assumption of continuity through death. But equally plainly he did not mean to satisfy the curiosity of men about the details of the life beyond. He would certainly have us believe that the constant sense of a world to come, where all the injustices of this world are to be rectified, and all the hypocrisies and secret things of this world are to come out into the light of God, is necessary to keep our faith firm and our hope clear and our love active. Equally certainly he would have men believe that they had in his present judgements of men and things the judgements of God, and that it is he who is to be the final judge. These are convictions which make the deepest practical difference in men's attitude towards life and its opportunities and perils. But the satisfaction of an insatiable curiosity about the life beyond, and the relation of the living to the dead, is a quite different matter, and Jesus shows no disposition to provide this satisfaction. From this point of view it is not difficult to distinguish between an other-worldliness which is really Christian and one which is not.

The sort of other-worldliness which has made the Church in many ages indifferent to the miseries of men, and prepared to tolerate the grossest violation of the spirit of justice and brotherhood, even in a nominally Christian society, is as flatly contrary to the spirit of Jesus as anything could be. The Church, as Jesus intends it to be, exists as the representative in this world of the kingdom of God which is the kingdom of justice and brotherhood. And the sentence of the final judge of men is to be swift and awful upon those who are content to ignore the misery which they might, if they would, both recognize and remedy. "Inasmuch as ye did it not unto one of the least of these my brethren ye did it not unto me. Depart, ye cursed."

On the other hand, it is certainly true that Jesus never allows us to expect that the perfect society is to be attained in this world. He bids us believe indeed that nothing done in the cause of God, however much it seem to fail, will ever be really lost. But he bids us look for a constant struggle, and he prepares us for the fiercest strain upon our faith unto the end. When the day of God dawns, it will not be as the conclusion of a gradual development towards perfection here in the world. It is here in the world that the witness of the Kingdom has to be borne, and here amidst strenuous conflict that

THE TEACHING OF JESUS 127

the materials of the city of God have to be fashioned; but the perfect building is to come from above. It is by a new creative act of God—under a new heaven and upon a new earth—that the City of God is to stand at last foursquare. That is certainly the substance of the teaching of Jesus, and there is nothing in human experience which warrants the expectation that the forces of evil are ever going to be overcome by gradual improvement in the world of our present experience. But also the idea of the consummation of all things given to us in the New Testament, or from the lips of Jesus, is never that of our being carried away to a distant heaven, but of a return of the Son of Man to a recreated earth, when the kingdoms of this regenerated world shall become the kingdoms of God and of His Christ.

The purpose of this chapter has been to give in as objective and disinterested a manner as possible an account both of the method of Jesus' teaching and of its ethical content—and particularly on some subjects of recent discussion, to indicate how, if we try to be faithful to all the earliest evidence, we can arrive at really intelligible and coherent results.

CHAPTER IV

THE REJECTION AND CRUCIFIXION OF JESUS [1]

WE have to take up the story of Jesus from the moment when Simon Peter, the spokesman and leader of the Twelve, resolutely, under the questioning of the Master, confessed him to be the Christ, and Jesus by welcoming the confession, and at the same time forbidding its publication beyond their own circle, made it to be the solemn secret which was to bind them to one another and to himself. This was the bright ending of the first epoch of their training, but it was also the beginning of another which was to lead to disaster. For no sooner had the Twelve committed themselves to the belief that he was the Christ, than Jesus began to press down on them the assurance that he was on the way to Jerusalem to be there rejected by the rulers of his people and put to death. This dismal forecast was renewed again and again. We find that Jesus endeavoured to reassure their

[1] Mark viii. 31 to xv., Luke ix. 22 to xxiii. 50.

THE CRUCIFIXION OF JESUS 129

minds, partly by convincing them that the Scriptures—no doubt especially the picture of the Suffering Servant from the later Isaiah, " led as a lamb to the slaughter "—should have made them receive such an intimation without dismay or surprise ; partly also by precise affirmations that the ignominy and the death were to be followed by resurrection and glory. But the attempted reassurances proved quite in vain— not indeed finally, for as seen in their ultimate issue they were indeed successful, but for the time. The very idea of a Christ who, instead of moving forward to victory and triumph, with " the good hand of God " upon him, should be rejected and handed over to an ignominious death, was so utterly repugnant to their minds that they were quite unable to entertain the principle of glory through shame or life through death, whether in the case of Jesus or as a more general law of life ; and Jesus did indeed compare his disciples also to a company of men condemned to death, and carrying their crosses, behind their leader, to the place of execution. That Jesus fully sympathized with their instinctive feeling of repugnance to the cross, as to some thing unnatural, was shown later in Gethsemane and on the cross itself : it was shown even when he first heard Peter's passionate outburst,

"This be far from thee," by the warmth with which he repudiated the protest, which rang in his ears simply as an old temptation of Satan renewed. But he accepted failure and all its consequences as the will of his Father, and kept insisting that he was going to his death, finding always on the part of the Twelve the same inability to apprehend his meaning. This blank refusal of "the counsel of God" among those who were nearest and dearest to him must have made the last period of his life a time of awful isolation.

Among the reassurances addressed to the disciples which at the time proved ineffective, the incident of the Transfiguration held a prominent place in their memories. There was even within the circle of the Twelve an inner circle of three or four. Three of them—Peter, James, and John—were taken by Jesus "up into a high mountain"—a place of retirement for prayer, as Luke explains. There, while Jesus prayed, they fell asleep; but when they were quite awakened, they saw a vision. It was their Master glorified, and in conversation with two men, likewise glorified, whom they recognized as Moses and Elijah—the lawgiver and the prophet—who were speaking of his approaching decease at Jerusalem. And while

THE CRUCIFIXION OF JESUS 131

these two forms were vanishing, and Peter was making a childish attempt to retain them, an awful cloud enveloped the disciples, and a voice out of the cloud bade them listen to Jesus, as to someone better than lawgiver or prophet— " This is my only son, hear him." And as the voice sounded, they found themselves alone with Jesus, and were forbidden to tell anyone what they had seen " save when the Son of Man is risen again from the dead."

We are told that in visions the subconscious mind of the subject supplies the scenery of the vision : but certainly, if we have in the narrative of the Transfiguration the account of the apostles' experiences which they later gave to their friends, the *substance* of the vision—that Jesus' words were to be utterly trusted and that death and glory were not incompatible —was not a subjective product, but a lesson from outside so alien to their own minds that they were at the time quite unable to assimilate it. The glorious vision of the Transfiguration is closely linked on the one hand to Peter's confession which precedes it, and on the other to the terrible scene of the demoniac, in face of whom the disciples, left below by Jesus and his three companions, found themselves utterly helpless. The sharp contrast between the glory of the mountain and the horror and shame of the plain have been made famous in art by Raphael's well-known picture of the Transfiguration.

After that we have in St. Luke's Gospel a long section (ix. 31—xix. 28), which seems throughout to be describing incidents in the final journey of Jesus to Jerusalem. This is suggested by frequent phrases. " It came to pass, when the days were well nigh come that he should be received up, he steadfastly set his face to go to Jerusalem " : " and as they went on the way " : " to cities and villages whither he himself was about to come " : " now as they went on their way " : " And he went on his way through cities and villages, teaching and journeying on to Jerusalem " : " As they were on the way to Jerusalem " : " Now there went with him great multitudes and he turned and said " : " As they were on the way to Jerusalem " : " Behold we go up to Jerusalem " : " As he drew nigh unto Jericho " : " He was passing through Jericho " : " He went on before going up to Jerusalem " : " When he drew nigh unto Bethphage and Bethany " : " When he drew nigh, he saw the city." The impression conveyed in Luke's narrative is unmistakable. But when we examine the narrative closely, we see that in fact it cannot all refer

THE CRUCIFIXION OF JESUS 133

to one journey. For instance, a journey to Jerusalem through Samaria could not be the same journey as one which brought Jesus by the Jordan valley to Jericho. We must admit that the three first Gospels, taken singly or taken together, are somewhat baffling documents to anyone who is seeking precise chronological or geographical information. That is not their object. But considered with reference to the spiritual purpose of Jesus' mission the sequence of incidents, parables and instructions contained in these chapters of St. Luke is highly illuminating.

At the beginning Jesus on his progress appears as sending disciples to prepare a Samaritan village to receive him; and they are repulsed because he was on his way to the abhorred city of Jerusalem. James and John, then, are furious, and wanted permission—" Sons of Thunder " as they were—to call fire down, as Elijah did, upon the insolent villagers; but Jesus rebuked them and simply turned aside to another village. If the famous words " Ye know not what manner of spirit ye are of "[1] must really, as a result of the study of the earliest manuscripts, be pronounced to be a later addition to the narrative, it must be ad-

[1] Luke ix. 55—omitted in R.V

mitted that the scribe, who penned this gloss upon the text, had very clear insight into the grounds of Jesus' rebuke, and very clear perception of the relation of the New Testament to the Old. It would be well indeed if the Church generally had retained this insight, especially with reference to the imprecatory psalms.

In what follows Jesus appears still in progress and appointing as many as seventy disciples to go, two and two together, as heralds of his approach to this village or that. They are to go, like the Twelve at an earlier date, making a certain royal claim, invested with a share in the miraculous powers of the Master and with his authority. "He that heareth you, heareth me; he that rejecteth you, rejecteth me: and that rejecteth me rejecteth him that sent me." We notice that Luke transfers to this Mission of the Seventy a good deal that St. Matthew's Gospel attaches to the earlier mission of the Twelve, making no mention at all of the later one. Now where you find in the same Gospel two very closely similar incidents, it is natural that critical students should regard them as " doublets "—that is, slightly differing reports of the same incident—supposing that the Evangelist received them from different

THE CRUCIFIXION OF JESUS 135

sources and took them mistakenly for reports of different events. Thus when we find in St. Mark a Feeding of Four Thousand side by side with a Feeding of Five Thousand, practically identical in all respects except in the numbers, it is natural to suppose that the one is a doublet of the other. And so in the case of the two Missions—one of the Twelve and one of the Seventy—mentioned by Luke, critics have suggested that Luke took from Mark, as he obviously did, his account of the first, but received his account of the second from some other source, and attached to it matter which he found in the document of the Lord's discourses, common to him and to St. Matthew; whereas in fact the story of the Mission of the Seventy is only another account of the Mission of the Twelve, exaggerated in respect of the number sent. In this case, however, the theory of the doublet is less convincing than in the case of the miraculous feedings. It has been worth while to pause in order to notice this theory, but we cannot stop to discuss it. It does not seriously matter whether there were really two distinct missions or only one, or whether, as is possible, there were numerous missions with varying numbers.

At any rate to the return of the Seventy

Luke, we notice, transfers, what in St. Matthew is attached more closely to that of the Twelve, the words of solemn thanksgiving, addressed by Jesus to his Father, because it has been His good pleasure that the Gospel should be acceptable not to the learned but to the " babes." It is followed by the solemn assurance of his divine commission to speak in his Father's name, and of his divine sonship, in virtue of which he and the Father stand over against one another in perfect mutual knowledge.[1] These momentous words stood, we must notice, in the earliest document of the Lord's discourses common to Matthew and Luke.

A large number of the parables and stories which have fastened themselves most deeply in the memory of mankind occur only in this section of Luke's Gospel (side by side with matter occurring also in Matthew's Gospel). Such specially Lucan passages are the stories of the Good Samaritan, the Rich Fool, the Pharisee and Publican at prayer in the Temple, and Dives and Lazarus; also the parables of the Barren Fig Tree, the Guests at the Feast, the Unjust Steward, the Lost Sheep, and the Prodigal Son. There are besides the narratives of Martha and Mary, of the Conversion of Zac-

[1] Matthew xi. 25 ff.; Luke x. 21 ff.

THE CRUCIFIXION OF JESUS 137

chæus, and the Healing of the Ten Lepers, among whom only one—a Samaritan—was found to be grateful. These passages bring out into the highest relief in the picture of Jesus his hatred of accumulated riches, and of pride and selfishness and narrow patriotism, his love of humility and brotherly service and of devotion to the word of God, and (it must be added) to himself. They can be for ever read and for ever appreciated with a fresh zest, and it is needless to repeat them.

But there are two passages, before we come to Jesus' arrival at Jerusalem, of which special note must be taken. One describes the peremptory refusal by Jesus of the offers to "follow him" made by certain men, who at the same time asked for a little delay, on what we should call the most reasonable grounds of domestic duty (ix. 57–62); the other gives us the strangely repellent utterance of Jesus when he turned on the crowds who followed him and said, "If any man cometh unto me and hateth not his own father, and mother, and wife, and children, and brethren and sisters, yea, and his own life also, he cannot be my disciple . . . whosoever there be of you who renounceth not all that he hath, he cannot be my disciple" (xiv. 25–33). We may, of course, in explanation of these passages, call attention to the practice of Jesus to express things in extremes, and call attention also to the Hebrew use of " loving " and " hating " as meaning " preferring " and " postponing." But to get at the heart of the matter we need to see something peculiar to the situation of the moment. Jesus is convinced that his people, as a body, will not accept him. He has come unto his own and his own have not received him. He is on his way to death. His term here is very short. He is looking to an immediate future beyond his own death, when his work must be carried on by others. For this tremendous task he is preparing a body of disciples, and they are chiefly the Twelve, the apostles. This is the small body to whom he says, " Fear not, little flock : it is my Father's good pleasure to give you the kingdom." This small body then must be of· the sort who are ready to face anything, even death itself. They must be stripped bare of all natural ties and anxieties and scruples, as thorough-going in their renunciation of the world as Francis of Assisi's Mendicant Friars. As we shall see, Jesus in the result got what he wanted, though not without a first failure, when the strain on the disciples' courage proved too great and their faith failed.

THE CRUCIFIXION OF JESUS 189

Ultimately, however, he got what he wanted, as we see in the record of the Apostles at the beginning of the Acts. But on his journey to Jerusalem for the last time, Jesus was determined that his body of disciples—his weapon for the future which he was fashioning and tempering and polishing—should be restricted to those who were prepared to give all for all and were totally free from all obligations to family and society. At the same period he could bless Zacchæus who, though in the hour of his conversion he dealt very freely with his property, yet did not give it all up; and he could send back those whom he healed to their home and friends. But however truly such persons might prove to be of his spirit and his Father's spirit, they were not of the chosen band which was to be his instrument. And the peremptory and absolute claim for actual renunciation of all other ties than one was reserved, it would seem, for these—upon whom all his plans and hopes for the great future were concentrated. This is the secret of his stern repudiation of all offers to " follow him " which were in any way qualified.

We are now on the verge of the entry of Jesus into Jerusalem—the moment of seeming triumph—and the passion, and death which

140 JESUS OF NAZARETH

follow. But there is one scene—which Mark inserts within the week of the Passion, but which John, in correction of Mark, expressly puts "six days before the Passover," and therefore probably on the Saturday before the triumphal entry—which demands notice. It is the scene in which the woman, whom John identifies with Mary the sister of Martha and Lazarus, lavishes upon the feet of Jesus in the course of a supper, the precious pistachio ointment which commanded a high price in the market. The disciples who were present, at the instigation of Judas, protested against such waste, and declared that the ointment ought to have been sold and the proceeds given to the poor. But Jesus defended the woman—" The poor ye have always with you . . . but me ye have not always. She hath done what she could; in that she poured this ointment upon my body, she did it to prepare my body for its approaching burial." Then with the vision before his eyes of the Gospel being preached in the whole world, he declared that this woman's act should be known wherever it went. This scene demands special notice, partly because it shows us vividly how the mental gaze of Jesus was fixed upon the wide horizon of the future, partly because it emphasizes that the meek and humble teacher

THE CRUCIFIXION OF JESUS 141

who took so calmly every insult, was at the same time deeply conscious of a divine worth such as rendered this expression of a woman's homage and devotion altogether acceptable and commendable.

Jesus was now indeed to present himself publicly for the first time in his royal dignity. The chosen occasion of the public display was the approach of the Passover festival, which year by year brought crowds from Galilee, as from all the world of the Jewish dispersion, to Jerusalem and its immediate neighbourhoodl Jesus was staying, and continued to stay til. the following Thursday evening, at the house of his friends at Bethany. But he had, it appears, other friends at the capital, for St. John tells us he had visited it several times before. Among these were presumably the owners of the young ass (upon which he rode, as the Messianic king described by Zachariah) who gave the animal up so readily, as soon as they heard that it was for the use of the Master. Such was probably also the owner of the house with the upper chamber, who gave it up for the use of Jesus and his disciples, according to what appears to have been a preconcerted arrangement. Again, though Jesus no doubt would have been widely known among the Galilæan pilgrims, yet the precise accounts of the procession suggest that there must have been previous preparation such as would have needed the co-operation of regular inhabitants of Jerusalem. It must, however, be acknowledged that St. John gives the whole incident a new verisimilitude by calling attention to the miracle of the Raising of Lazarus as its immediate occasion. That had created a special excitement, a concentration of interest upon Jesus.

The story of the Entry had best be read in the Gospel. It was a moment of public triumph —planned perhaps *for* Jesus, but certainly also *by* him deliberately accepted and directed; and it was a public assertion of his Messiahship which Jesus refused to rebuke or suppress; it was a scene of enthusiasm shared by the company who came with him from Bethany and by the crowd—probably mostly Galilæans—who came out to meet him from within the city walls. The scene of joy is only interrupted when Jesus paused at the first sight of Jerusalem across the Kedron valley—when he " beheld the city and wept over it," and spoke the memorable words of doom and lamentation over it.

It is plain that the welcome which Jesus received was sufficiently widespread and obvious

THE CRUCIFIXION OF JESUS 143

to make his adversaries, both Sadducees and Pharisees, seriously alarmed, and also to impress them with the necessity for caution. Thus they did not think it prudent, either that Sunday or on the following days, to arrest him in public, while at the same time they—especially the high priests' family and party—were determined that his career should be brought to a speedy end. We must follow with some precision the events of the last days. Mark's narrative is the best to follow, supplemented, however, occasionally by Luke and by John's corrections and additions, which are here especially important and convincing.

Jesus, on the Sunday, finished his public entry at the Temple, but only looked round on what he saw and withdrew to Bethany for the night.

The next morning early he went again towards the Temple, but on his way wrought his one recorded miracle of judgement. In the hearing of his disciples he solemnly doomed to perpetual fruitlessness a fig tree, which by its early clothing of leaves gave the promise of some sort of food which could have satisfied the hunger of Jesus. (There appears to be present-day evidence that the peasantry can and do feed upon the green knops which break out early upon the twigs of fig trees.) Then he went on his way; and it was only the following day that the disciples drew his attention to the fact that the fig tree had already withered. Mark's account is a very precise account of the order of events, and the miracle is no doubt so carefully recorded on account of its obvious symbolism. It was an acted parable of judgement on Jerusalem—so splendid and so disappointing.

On his entry into the outer courts of the Temple Jesus found the Temple market in full play, as would have been the case especially at festival time. The people had to buy beasts and birds for sacrifice, and those destined for sacrifice had to be certified as sound by the priestly scrutineers before they could be offered. No doubt those sold in the Temple market had already been "passed," and the people found it convenient to buy there : moreover the money to be paid in the Temple, whether for the purchase of victims or for the temple tribute, must be Palestinian money free from Pagan symbols; so the pilgrims coming from many countries had to change their various moneys, which was another source of profit. Presumably the high-priests (the family of Annas) got a large share of these profits. We

THE CRUCIFIXION OF JESUS 145

hear in Jewish documents of the "Bazaar of the Sons of Annas," which was a public scandal. It is tempting to identify this with the Temple market; and to suppose that, while the family did not want to come out into the open in defence of a recognized scandal, they were determined to maintain it. But the evidence about the "Bazaar" would seem to point to the Mount of Olives as its site, and it is well not to be too imaginative.

It is a mistake to treat the act of Jesus in driving the buyers and sellers and money changers out of the court of the Temple as a resort on his part to physical violence, even though he used the whip mentioned by John. There is not the least reason to suppose that the little band of Jesus and his disciples could have offered effective opposition to the marketers, if they had chosen to resist. The triumphant act of Jesus was an act of moral authority. They could not stand before his blazing indignation against such a defilement of his Father's House, the House of Prayer. It should be noted that there is no ground for attributing to Jesus any other motive for his action (such as a horror of animal sacrifices). It is possible that the market was only held, or was only a conspicuous scene, on the occasion of festivals. But it is noticeable that there is no mention of Passover lambs among the animals exposed for sale. John, who at several points corrects Mark's story, records a similar incident quite at the beginning of Jesus' career, but is quite silent about it at this point. It is not his general habit to repeat the story of Mark, which he takes for granted, and he probably meant us to understand that the same action was twice taken. This may well have been the case: but, if we had to choose between the two dates, we should choose Mark's. The Chief Priests, with their Temple guard at their disposal, were no doubt furious; but in face of the enthusiasm for Jesus so strikingly shown a day before, they determined not to arrest him in public.

Jesus therefore returned unmolested to the Temple and taught day after day. The sequel of incidents recorded by Mark, and reproduced by Luke as well as by Matthew, is extraordinarily impressive. Jesus' rejoinder to the chief priests and others, who question his authority, by another question about the authority of John the Baptist, which they are quite unable to answer, is masterly. It is followed by the parable of the vineyard which intimates plainly enough that their authority in the vineyard of God (Israel) is to be brought to an end

THE CRUCIFIXION OF JESUS 147

and the vineyard handed over to new management. Then he is confronted by the Pharisees and Herodians in alliance, to seek to get from him such an answer about paying the imperial tribute as, one way or the other, would get him into trouble; and again his response, though in effect it is a response in favour of paying, is such as to silence them. Then confronted by difficulties about the Resurrection, raised by the Sadducees, he speaks plain and illuminating words about the life beyond, unambiguously affirming the resurrection against the Sadducees, ridding it of the materialistic associations of a mere resuscitation of the flesh, and arguing that the personal relation to a living God, in which the Patriarchs of Israel are presented to us in the Old Testament, must be a permanent relation. Here he won the cordial assent of " some of the scribes "—no doubt the Pharisaic scribes.

Then one of them, impressed by his wisdom, draws from him his great affirmation that the first and great commandment of the love of God, and the second that is like to it of the love of one's fellow man, constitute the ground and summary of " the whole law and the prophets " : after which no further questions are ventured. But Jesus takes the initiative and cross-questions the Pharisees about their description of the Christ who is to come as " the Son of David." He quotes one of the Psalms assigned to David, and asks how the inspired king can have hailed as Lord (" Jehovah said unto *my Lord* ") one who was merely his son ? To this there was no answer ; and Jesus seems to have asked the question not with the intention of denying that the Christ was to be David's son, but merely to make them feel that their glib answer was not adequate. He loved to make men " think again " what their own professed principles involved.

There is a notable phrase used by Luke of these days when Jesus was teaching daily in the Temple—" the people all hung upon him listening." It was in " the hearing of all the people " thus " hanging upon him " that Jesus solemnly warned his disciples against the scribes on account of their ostentation, vanity, covetousness and hypocrisy. But the long series of woes denounced upon " the Scribes and Pharisees " for these and other vices, which occurs in St. Matthew at this point, is given by Luke in a shorter form, at an earlier date and on a more private occasion—in the house of a Pharisee who had asked him to dinner. There can be no doubt, however, that Jesus did denounce the religious teachers of Israel for these vices,

THE CRUCIFIXION OF JESUS 149

after the manner of the ancient prophets. It was a declaration of open war. It must be admitted also that there is no sign of discrimination in the reports we have of these denunciations. They are quite general—of the whole class. Dr. Klausner, the living Jewish author of *Jesus of Nazareth*, while admitting that " much of this criticism was certainly justified," and quoting parallels to it from the Talmud, complains that " Jesus (or the tradition) errs by unfair generalization, by attributing to all Pharisees the defects of the few." It is of course possible that there was more discrimination in the words as Jesus spoke them. But St. Paul, who had been educated among them, implies the same sort of judgement upon the Jewish zealots of the law (Rom. ii. 17-24). Those who recognize how much the Christian Church has suffered in history from the arrogance, obscurantism, formalism and hypocrisy of great ecclesiastics, especially at certain epochs of history, cannot but be thankful that, in the ground documents of Christianity, this indignant denunciation of these vices stands on record. It was just what brought the Pharisees nearer to Jesus than the Sadducees—their real zeal for religion—which made their conspicuous faults more especially hateful to him.

150   JESUS OF NAZARETH

Following on the denunciations of Pharisaism, we find Jesus deliberately observing the contributions being made by the people to the Temple treasury, and we hear his memorable declaration of the supreme worth of the poor widow's " two mites." It is noticeable how in our day the common expression " I will give my mite " makes a claim for the Lord's approbation by those who are very far from giving " all their living " to the service of God.

As Jesus left the Temple to return to Bethany, perhaps on the Wednesday evening, one of the disciples—probably a Galilæan to whom Herod's magnificent Temple was a novel spectacle—called his attention to the vast stones of the structure and to its grandeur, but Jesus replied by a curt and emphatic prophecy that its total ruin was approaching. When the party of Jesus had reached the summit of Olivet on their way home, the two pairs of brothers, Peter and Andrew, and James and John, asked him privately when this should happen, and what signs would tell them when to expect it; and Jesus replied in what is called " the apocalyptic discourse " —intended apparently as a confidential communication to the Four—which has been the subject of endless controversy at different periods. For its elucidation in detail enquirers

THE CRUCIFIXION OF JESUS 151

must go to the commentaries. Here we must be content to recall what has been already said (pp. 114 ff.) about Jesus' apocalyptic teaching, and to summarize its contents very briefly thus— Jesus warns the disciples that they are to expect a period of profound agitation, political, physical and spiritual, during which they must steadfastly refuse to be led astray by lying rumours, or to give their confidence to false claimants, and must show a faith which no isolation or hatred or persecution can quench, while they steadily pursue the task of evangelizing the world. There is a great deal to be borne and done by them before " the end " can come. " The end " means, in the first instance, the event with which alone their question (as given by Mark and Luke) was concerned—the destruction of the Temple and of Jerusalem. That is an event which is certain to happen, Jesus tells them, within the experience of men already alive. No false patriotism must lead astray the disciples of Jesus. They—that is, the disciples in Jerusalem—must be ready at once to forsake the city and flee, as soon as they witness what Mark describes in cryptic terms derived from the book of Daniel, but Luke interprets in plain language as " Jerusalem compassed with armies." For Jerusalem is irreversibly doomed, and their attitude towards all " patriotic " hopes is to be one of absolute detachment. Then (after the manner of the ancient prophets) this doom on Jerusalem is shown on the background of a vast and lurid catastrophe affecting the whole world, the final " day of judgement." That day, when God is to come into His own, is surely to dawn upon a terrified world : but as to *when* that day and that hour is to be Jesus declares that the Father only knows—no man, not even the highest angel, not the Son himself. Only at all times they must be ready for the ultimate event and watchful for its coming.

As to the significance of this " apocalyptic " expectation, as much has been said above as this short study of Jesus' teaching admits of. In Matthew's collection of the Lord's sayings two memorable parables—the Wise and Foolish Virgins and the Talents—illustrate the duty of watchfulness, and the sequence closes with the unforgettable picture of the final judgement of all the races of mankind by the " Son of Man," in which the great verdict of final acceptance or rejection of individuals is pronounced, to the astonishment of both sections alike, in accordance with their active kindness, or their apathy, in presence of the suffering and distress

THE CRUCIFIXION OF JESUS 153

of those whom Jesus calls "my brethren"; for to help them has been to help him, and to ignore them to ignore him.

At an earlier stage Jesus is described in St. Matthew's Gospel as fulfilling Isaiah's prophecy of the Servant of Jehovah who " shall not strive, nor cry aloud; neither shall anyone hear his voice in the streets. A bruised reed shall he not break, and smoking flax shall he not quench, till he send forth judgement unto victory." But now at the end, in the challenge to the Sadducees and the open denunciation of the Pharisees, the " still small voice " was superseded by the thunders of judgement from the lips of Jesus. The thundering, however, is soon over. In the last scenes of the Upper Chamber and Gethsemane, and the Trial and Calvary, Jesus appears only in tender care and sympathy towards his weak-hearted disciples, and towards his adversaries in the dignity of meek endurance.

It would appear that Jesus now perceived that his hour was actually come. He had detected the treasonable design in the heart of his only Judæan apostle, Judas of Karioth. If, as seems certainly the case, John is correct in putting the Passover feast of the Jews on the Friday night *after* the Crucifixion, and not, as appears on the surface of the other accounts, on the previous Thursday evening, then we may interpret Jesus' saying at the supper-table, " With desire I have desired to eat this Passover with you before I suffer " as an expression of what had been his earnest wish, which he now saw was destined to be frustrated. Judas, he knows, would act, and, with his help, the chief priests would act, before the Passover. Such in fact was their intention, but they were afraid of a popular tumult. Probably they overrated the loyalty of the Galilæan crowd, whom Jesus had again disappointed by taking no action to assert himself, as the Christ-King of their imagination would have done, after the " good beginning " of the Entry and the Cleansing of the Temple. But Judas showed them the way. What exactly was it that he betrayed ? The Entry had been a public announcement that Jesus was the Messiah, and in that announcement he clearly took part. The former secret was now out. It cannot have been *that* which Judas betrayed. He can have betrayed only enough of Jesus' intentions and habits to enable the chief priests to take him in a quiet solitary place at night, where no disturbance could arise, and to get him condemned and made away with before the Feast. The character of

THE CRUCIFIXION OF JESUS 155

Judas is described in the Gospels with a terrible simplicity. He was a shrewd business man who loved money, and he found the utter indifference of Jesus to all considerations of "prudence" intolerable; his contempt of money he could not endure. Whether he was such a miser as simply to have been overcome by the proffered bribe, or whether (as the Gospels do not in the least suggest) there was present a more subtle motive—to drive Jesus to extremities, with the idea that at the last he would be obliged to assert himself and use his miraculous powers to sustain his cause—it is idle to enquire. It may be mentioned, however, that the exact sum, "thirty pieces of silver," specified only by St. Matthew as paid to Judas, is probably only a reflection from the ancient prophet Zachariah's words (Zach. xi. 12) about the price paid by Israel to its "shepherd" for his services—the price fixed in the Law of Moses as compensation for a slave.

Jesus then, anticipating how things would go, did not return to the city from Bethany on Thursday morning, but sent two of his disciples, who, in accordance with what looks like previous arrangements made with a friendly householder, were to make provision for a supper in a roomy upper chamber, which could not be

156 JESUS OF NAZARETH

properly the Passover meal, but which in the earliest days of the Church gained that character. It gained it because of its association with the institution of the Eucharist, which was regarded as the new and true paschal celebration; as St. Paul wrote, " Christ our Passover has been sacrificed for us : therefore let us keep the feast." Such a religious meal—now to be a farewell meal—was probably a familiar rite of the brotherhood of Jesus, and was in accordance with Jewish custom. The washing of the feet of his disciples by Jesus, which only John records, must have occurred at the beginning; perhaps in connection with the painful struggle for precedence among the disciples, which Luke mentions. Then after the last cup of the supper—the one cup of which they all drank —Jesus instituted a new rite, which he bequeathed to his disciples to practise after he had gone. It was to be a rite in commemoration of his death, which he was to offer to God as the sacrifice by which the New Covenant of God with Israel was to be inaugurated. The mysterious " words of institution " come to us first from St. Paul, where he recalls to the Corinthians that he had delivered this account to them on his first coming among them, as part of the tradition which he himself " received "

THE CRUCIFIXION OF JESUS 157

when he was converted—only a short time after the Crucifixion. By that time then the tradition of the institution was fixed. The account of it which St. Paul recites is confirmed by Mark, and later by Matthew, who probably gives us the tradition of Northern Palestine. If anything about Jesus is good history that must be. What meaning the disciples can have attached *at the moment* to this mysterious language about eating the body of Jesus after his death and drinking his blood, we cannot tell. But in fact Jesus was taking measures in view of a future date, when their intelligences would have been astonishingly deepened and opened, as we shall see.

It seems to the present writer that the discourses of Jesus to his disciples, begun at the supper-table, which St. John records[1]—so intimately arising out of the situation of the moment viewed in the light of the immediate future —again, so different from anything we can reasonably ascribe to early Christian invention— and, once more, so necessary to interpret the eager expectation of the Holy Spirit which the disciples showed a few weeks later—those discourses of Jesus must be in substance authentic. They were to prepare the bewildered disciples

[1] John xiv-xvii.

for his leaving them—orphans for a little while —and then for his return, in a manner quite different to what their imaginations would have suggested, by the sending of the Holy Spirit. At these last moments Jesus impressed them with a sense of something mysterious about his person, about his relation to "the Father" and his future relation to them, which at the time their bewildered minds could not and did not grasp, but which was to remain imprinted on their memories until the strange happenings of the next days or weeks should have given them the clue. Of all this we must think later. Now we must follow along with the story of the disciples as they were—still quite unilluminated—and of their Master.

The picture of Gethsemane is by universal consent one of the most moving pictures of human history. The prophets and Psalmists of old Israel and the supreme poet of the Book of Job had given perhaps more powerful and constant expression than is to be found anywhere else in literature to the horror of the righteous soul at the spectacle of triumphant evil, and the bewildered agony of the believing mind at the seeming indifference of God. All this horror and agony are here seen possessing the soul of Jesus. His spirit is free from the sense of sin.

THE CRUCIFIXION OF JESUS

He has wholly sought the Father's will. He has served to the uttermost for the needs of men. Now he looks around and finds himself deserted and alone. He looks forward and sees what is to happen. Those in whose hands he is are moving wholly under the power of the Evil One. All that he must bear—the death he must die—is a hideous anomaly. So he pleads in agony of soul against the monstrous horror of it all, while at the same time his human will holds on its allotted way in flawless obedience. "Father, if it be possible, let this cup pass from me. Nevertheless, not my will, but thine be done." Surely the author of the Epistle to the Hebrews is right when he finds the supreme moment of spiritual strain and trial, not on the Cross, but in Gethsemane. Anticipation is often a greater strain than actual endurance. So it was when Jesus " offered up strong crying and tears unto Him that was able to save him from death, and having been heard for his godly fear, though he was a Son yet learned obedience (the greatest of all lessons) from the things that he suffered." Three times he prayed in agony and three times he found his most intimate friends asleep. But the struggle is over. He stands now composed, and so remains to the end.

Perhaps, however, this scene was not altogether without a witness who was awake. There are two strange verses in Mark's Gospel about a young man in a linen garment who was a witness of the capture of Jesus and barely managed to escape. It is quite likely that he was also a witness of the preceding moment of his agonized prayer. For the introduction of his adventure there is no imaginable motive unless it is Mark's way of saying, " I was there myself." We know that he was the son of the woman whose house was the Christian centre in Jerusalem fifteen years later. Was not " the upper chamber," which was the home of the Apostles immediately after the experiences of the Ascension, perhaps in the same house ? Was it not probably the scene also of the Last Supper ? Might not the young son of the house have followed the group furtively from the chamber to Gethsemane ? Is there any other reasonable explanation of those otherwise quite meaningless verses in St. Mark ?

The record of the seizure of Jesus by the Temple guard under the guidance of Judas needs no comment, save on one point—the attempt of Peter to use the sword, which Jesus instantly rebuked—" He that takes the sword, shall perish by the sword." An hour before Jesus

THE CRUCIFIXION OF JESUS 161

had told the disciples that the moment had come for them to sell their garments and buy swords; and they had shown him two which they had already, and he had said, "It is enough." Jesus never appears to have allowed himself in anything like making a joke. But he seems occasionally to speak ironically; and he must surely have done so on this occasion. The two swords would have been of no use in any case to defend the disciples, and the first attempt to use them was promptly rebuked.

The four accounts of the trials are discrepant in details. But if we take Mark's account as our basis and admit added details and corrections on minor points from Luke and John, the successive examinations and charges and condemnations stand out clearly. All the accounts, as well of the trials as of the subsequent Passion of Jesus, are marked by a wonderful sobriety and restraint. There are no outbursts of indignant feeling on the part of the recorders, and no dwelling on physical horrors. The effect is as wonderful an instance of impressiveness through simplicity as is to be found in literature. The figure of Jesus stands in the midst with a majesty which confound his adversaries and triumphs over ignominy and insults.

Jesus is first taken to Annas' house for a

162　JESUS OF NAZARETH

preliminary examination which would have been probably before midnight. When Luke reckons Annas and Caiaphas both as high-priests he is speaking inexactly. Caiaphas alone was high-priest, but Annas his father-in-law, the head of the family and former high-priest, exercised influence in the background. After the preliminary examination in his house, at which Jesus claimed justice, and after the customary rough treatment of the prisoner which accompanied it, he is taken from Annas to Caiaphas—probably to the official residence of the high-priest, which may have been close by—and there in the early morning a trial took place before the Sanhedrin. Comment has often been made on all the irregularities which occurred in the proceedings, as judged by the rules of procedure which we find in the later Mishna. But the treatise concerned with the Sanhedrin comes from a date long after A.D. 29, when circumstances were quite different. We cannot tell what rules had been formulated at the date with which we are concerned. At this trial the object appears to have been to fasten upon Jesus the charge of blasphemy. It is curious that the accusation made by the two " false witnesses "—that he said, " I will destroy this temple which is made with hands and

THE CRUCIFIXION OF JESUS 163

in three days I will raise another made without hands "—was nearly *verbally* true (according to John ii. 19). What he had in fact said was "Destroy this temple" (i.e. Let this material house of God be destroyed) "and I will quickly raise up a better spiritual shrine." But Jesus did not explain. Doubtless this was an example of wisdom. A precise explanation to such an audience would only have sounded like quibbling. As it was, the evidence was set aside as "not equal," which seems to mean "not adequate." It has to be remembered that there were probably a few among the judges who were of the mind of Joseph of Arimathæa, or of Nicodemus, and desired just treatment for Jesus; and the fiercer spirits among them had to keep within bounds. Finally Caiaphas put the prisoner on his oath, and demanded an answer to a direct question whether he claimed to be the Christ. Whether Jesus' reply was "Thou sayest it" (an ambiguous answer) or the direct "I am" (as to which the accounts differ), at any rate he went on to use words which unmistakably implied that he did. His profession was in effect that henceforth they should see Daniel's vision fulfilled: they should see the sovereignty of the Son of Man realized. That was enough for Caiaphas. "What need we any further witness ? He has claimed to be the Christ. What does this claim amount to ? It is sheer blasphemy. What is your verdict and what is to be the punishment ? " And the judges demanded the death-sentence. Though there was no formal definition of blasphemy which included the claim to be Messiah, it may be argued that there was really no alternative between accepting the claim or condemning the claimant. The brutal treatment of the condemned prisoner was probably customary in all courts at the time. But Mark's statement that "all the judges condemned him to be guilty of death" cannot be strictly true, if Joseph of Arimathæa was among them.

It is hard to endure reading the account of the disciples' conduct. Judas' treachery is disgusting enough, however it is sought to explain it. The cowardice of the whole group, who, when Jesus was arrested, " forsook him and fled," seems despicable. But if the statement is exact, two at least recovered themselves and followed to Annas' house or to the scene of the later trial—John, who was known to the household of the high-priest, and Peter. There, at some point in the proceedings, Peter was charged three times over with being of Jesus' company, and three times denied it, at

THE CRUCIFIXION OF JESUS 165

last on his oath—" So help me God, I know nothing about the man." The story in Mark is probably Peter's own. If, as we read it, it stings like a whip even to this day, it is because we recognize how weak human nature is, when a man's faith has failed and he finds himself alone among enemies.

The Sanhedrin recognized that they could not carry out the death-sentence for themselves, and must carry the case at once before the Procurator, who because it was the festival time, when Jerusalem was crowded, and trouble might occur, was in the city, occupying probably Herod's palace. The Jews could not enter " the Prætorium," for they had to retain their " purity " in order to be able in the evening to keep the Passover. Jesus therefore is taken inside, but Pilate has to come out to deal with the Jews. It is to be remembered that Pilate had already a bad record for irritating the Jews; that was not the policy of Rome, so long as a subject people was not endangering Roman sovereignty. As matters stood, we may say that he would have felt it to be more than his place was worth to resist the demand of the priests for the condemnation of Jesus. Of course they had to frame an indictment such as a Roman magistrate would take cognizance

166   JESUS OF NAZARETH

of. (The Acts gives us a vivid picture of their indifference to religious questions, or questions of Church law among the Jews. Gallio's or Festus' attitude towards such questions was typical.) Luke tells us that the indictment of Jesus by the representatives of the Sanhedrin was threefold—that he "perverted the nation" or led them in ways dangerous to the authorities : that he condemned payment of the imperial taxes : and that he called himself King of the Jews." Pilate was obviously anxious to get rid of the prisoner. He tried to get the Jews to take the case back to their own court, but they replied that the case demanded the death sentence, which they could not execute. Then, hearing that Jesus' career as a teacher had begun in Galilee, he tried to get him off upon Herod, who was also in Jerusalem. Herod, as we know, was perturbed in his mind about Jesus. He was reported to have described him as "John the Baptist over again." When Jesus had crossed to Peræa, he had tried apparently to get rid of him by frightening him with information of a design on his part to put him also to death as he had done John, and Jesus had sent him a sharp reply and called him "the fox" (which Klausner recognizes as an apt description). Herod was also a superstitious

THE CRUCIFIXION OF JESUS 167

man, curious about Jesus' reputation as a miracle-worker, and "he hoped to see some miracle done by him." But before him Jesus refused to make any answer at all to the vehement accusations of the Jews: and Herod, no doubt anxious to avoid responsibility in a difficult case, about which feelings ran high in Galilee, allowed his soldiers to deride him as a mock king, but sent him back to Pilate, saying probably that he could make nothing of him and that it was a case for the Imperial Government to act.

So Pilate finds himself in a situation where he must do something. Conversation with the prisoner within convinces him that Jesus is concerned in no enterprise which could be of any danger to the Empire. He was an enthusiast about unknowable matters such as practical governors had nothing to do with. He seems even to have gone out and announced to the Jews that neither he nor Herod found any ground for executing him, and he should release him. But outside he found a clamour. It came from two distinct groups which coalesced. There was a popular bandit called Barabbas who was in prison, and there was a custom that one prisoner should be let out on popular demand as an act of clemency at the Feast. There was a crowd demanding the liberation of Barabbas. He seems to have been a dangerous person, and Pilate tried to get them to ask for Jesus " your king " instead of Barabbas. But that was not at all a welcome proposal; and the crowd who demanded Barabbas coalesced with the chief-priests' crowd in demanding the execution of Jesus. Pilate brought out Jesus and showed him to them—a pitiful sight by this time, no doubt. "Behold the Man." But he was met only by howls. So Barabbas was released, and Jesus was given up to be subjected to the ignominious and agonizing punishment of crucifixion, which was the common Roman punishment for provincials whom they found dangerous, a very common punishment which excited no attention. Josephus' history is full of records of this form of execution—sometimes put in force on vast numbers of men.

In the Apocalypse "the city where Jesus was crucified" is identified "mystically" with Sodom and Egypt, which means that it is the worldly city wherever that appears. That is the truth. Men being what they were and are, the crucifixion of Jesus, when it occurred, had a certain inevitability. Christian Europe has often imagined that the Jews who caused Jesus to be crucified were abnormally wicked people. But

THE CRUCIFIXION OF JESUS 169

that is not so. He had challenged the Pharisees to change their fundamental ideas and methods in matters of religion; and when have high ecclesiastics been ready to accept this challenge from a " mere layman " ? He became in the eyes of the priestly family a source of danger to their position and their wealth, for he claimed, or allowed other people to claim for him, the title of King of the Jews, and he had attacked a valuable source of income—the Temple market —perhaps twice over. Again, he had offended all the patriotic prejudices of the nation. No zealot, no ordinary Jew on the look-out for the Messiah to come, could have a word to say for him, when they really understood what he meant by the Kingdom of God. As for Pilate, Roman justice was of a sort which did not care much for the rights of an individual provincial, if the imperial interests demanded that he should be got rid of. If, then, it was essential in the view of the Jewish leaders to silence that troublesome voice, and there was no considerable body to stand up for him, and Pilate was not prepared to make himself unpopular by resisting their demand, the result which actually followed was inevitable. And no one who watches human life on the large scale in history will deny that the motives which determined the crucifixion of

Jesus are the common human motives, and that in truth " the city where Jesus was crucified " is the worldly world all over.

The account of the crucifixion and entombment of Jesus should be read only in the Gospels. Its simplicity carries conviction for the most part and the discrepancies are insignificant—save that there are certain details given in Matthew only, especially as to mysterious occurrences occurring at the moment of Jesus' death and as to the sealing and watching of his tomb which almost all critical scholars regard as untrustworthy. Here we will content ourselves with a few notes on the incidents of the crucifixion.

" Scourging always preceded crucifixion : so Josephus twice informs us. This was a horrible punishment, reducing the naked body to strips of raw flesh and inflamed and bleeding weals. And when afterwards the victim's hands were nailed to the cross-piece and his feet tied or nailed to the base of the beam . . . nothing could have been more horrible or appalling." (Klausner). It was a mode of punishment which appears to have been invented by the Phœnicians and adopted by the Romans. It was intended to be as ignominious as possible, and the cruel horseplay of the Roman soldiery

THE CRUCIFIXION OF JESUS 171

was a fitting accompaniment. The spectacle of condemned men led out to suffer this punishment, bearing the cross-beam from which they were to hang, would have been familiar in Palestine. Jesus, however, was found too much exhausted to carry his own cross, and Simon, from Cyrene in North Africa, where there was a large Jewish colony, was enforced to carry it for him. The familiar way in which St. Mark —writing at Rome perhaps forty years after the crucifixion—names his sons, shows that the family had come to carry their cross and follow Jesus in a spiritual sense. The potion of drugged wine given to those about to be crucified was intended to dull their senses. It was a measure of mercy: "Wealthy women in Jerusalem," says the Talmud, "used to contribute these things and bring them." But Jesus chose to suffer with all his senses about him and would not drink it. The cross, we should notice, was not a lofty erection such as is generally represented in pictures. It only raised the head of the sufferer some foot and a half above that of the bystanders. Jesus could hear the jibes aimed at him and speak to John and his mother. The "title," a piece of wood covered with white gypsum, on which the nature of the condemned man's crime was written, was carried before him. As to the bare words " The King of the Jews," Klausner writes: " The sly tyrant could not resist the pleasure of jibing at the Jewish nation by means of an inscription above the cross : B old how we the Romans inflict the most ignominious of deaths upon the so-called King of the Jews." The crucifixion lasted from some time about nine in the morning till three in the afternoon.

In the foundation document (St. Mark) only one word of Jesus from the cross is recorded, uttered at the end of his sufferings, in which he adopted the agonized question of an ancient servant of God who found himself forsaken— " My God, my God, why didst thou desert me ? " By this tremendous question, which received no answer, he united himself to all the band of righteous souls who have been tortured in mind by the seeming indifference of God. Luke omits this question ; but he records another, also taken from the Psalms (which seem to have filled the mind of Jesus at the end), " Father, into thy hands I commend my spirit," indicating that the resolute endurance of unintelligible anguish and ignominy passed into the confidence of sonship. Luke and John record between them six words of Jesus, omitting the central question. There were possible wit-

THE CRUCIFIXION OF JESUS 173

nesses amongst the bystanders, such as Simon who carried the cross, and one or another of the women who stood by watching, who could have heard these words and reported them; and closely examined they have a marvellous verisimilitude. They all must have been spoken either in the earlier hours of the crucifixion—the prayer of Jesus for the pardon of his executioners, his generous welcome of the penitent bandit who hung beside him, and his brief arrangement for his mother's comfort—or quite at the end—the great question, the "I thirst," the "It is finished," and the commendation of his spirit into the hands of his Father.

The physical strength of Jesus was worn out before the crucifixion began, and he died upon the cross sooner than most of those who suffered this horrible death. When some soldiers—sent at the request of the Jews, who would not have the bodies remain upon the crosses in the sacred hours of the Sabbath, which was also the Passover festival—came to expedite the death of the three crucified men by breaking their legs, they found Jesus dead already. And John further reports that "one of them with a spear pierced his side, and straightway there came out blood and water." This he declares to be the testimony of an eye-witness. The other

Evangelists narrate that a great gloom settled on the earth from the sixth hour to the ninth, and at the ninth hour when Jesus died the veil in the Temple that covered the Holy of Holies was rent in the midst—by an earthquake, as St. Matthew adds. They all tell also how Joseph of Arimathæa, an honoured member of the Sanhedrin, well disposed to Jesus, who had refused to agree to his condemnation, went to Pilate and asked for the body of Jesus, and, having had his request granted, took it down from the cross and wrapped it in linen and laid it in a neighbouring tomb, hewn in the rock, " where never man had yet laid," and rolled a round stone to cover the entrance of the tomb. John adds that Nicodemus, another " ruler of the Jews," joined him in the entombment, and brought a supply of spices to insert in the wrappings. "And the women also," Luke adds, " which came with him from Galilee, followed after, and beheld the sepulchre, and how his body was laid."

CHAPTER V

ARE OUR GOSPELS TRUSTWORTHY?

1. *Prefatory Considerations*

So far we have been following the course of the life and teaching of Jesus from his first public appearance to his death upon the Cross. It is of course certain that the Christian Gospel, when it first went out into the world, was not based on the story of a life ending in a death, such as is the common lot of men. It centred upon Jesus raised from the dead and exalted to divine glory as Christ and Lord. Nevertheless it had its roots in the earlier experience. The Apostles, who presided over the new community at Jerusalem, were men who had been in the company of Jesus " all the time that he went in and went out among us, beginning from the baptism of John unto the day that he was received up." So Peter, at the beginning of the Acts, is reported as defining the requirement for a new Apostle to take the place of the traitor and suicide Judas. And later he is reported as saying that the witness of the

Apostles was to a certain "message which God sent unto the children of Israel, preaching peace by Jesus Christ. . . . That saying ye yourselves know, which was published throughout all Judæa (Palestine), beginning from Galilee, after the baptism which John preached; even Jesus of Nazareth, how that God anointed him with the Holy Spirit and with power: who went about doing good and healing all who were oppressed by the devil, for God was with him. And we are witnesses of all things which he did both in the country of the Jews and in Jerusalem: whom also they slew, hanging him on a tree." It is an altogether extravagant scepticism which can doubt that there was such a prophet as Jesus of Nazareth whose career had such a beginning in John's preaching, and that there was such a message claiming to be divine which was proclaimed by him in Palestine, and such a life of beneficent power lived which did end in his crucifixion, and finally that there was such a body of chosen witnesses left behind by Jesus to spread the good news of the Kingdom. So at this point we will pause, and before we examine the later substance of the Gospel we will face the question whether reasonable people to-day, after 1,900 years, can take the account of the life and ministry of Jesus, which we have got in the Gospels of Mark and Luke, as being substantially the account which the first witnesses, if we could have questioned them, would have given of their experiences, from the day they first joined his company down to his death upon the cross, and —what is of course a different question—whether we to-day can receive their testimony as true.

In our days, no person at all conversant with modern literature can approach this enquiry without anxiety. Probably our grandfathers, if not our fathers, were able to approach the Gospels with the conviction that their writers, like all the writers of the Bible, were supernaturally inspired, in the sense that the Holy Spirit directed and controlled their minds and even their pens so as to ensure infallible accuracy in what was written. The effort of the reader therefore was limited to finding out precisely what the words meant : their meaning, even in details, must be taken to be God's word and not merely man's witness. There are important bodies in our day—the authorities in the Roman Catholic Church and the Fundamentalists among the Protestants—who still hold to the doctrine : but most of us have been obliged to abandon it simply because it seems to be disproved by the facts. The position is this—the earliest account given us of the origin of St. Mark's Gospel is given (about A.D. 130) by a certain Papias, Bishop of Hierapolis. He writes somewhat disparagingly of written records altogether, and for himself prefers the living voice of the first witnesses, "the elders" as he calls them, as reported to him by their immediate followers, who were still accessible to him in his earlier years. Then in a fragment of his writings which survives he gives this account of St. Mark's Gospel, as he had received it from one of these elders:

> "This also the elder said : Mark, having become the interpreter of Peter, wrote down accurately everything that he remembered of the things which were either said or done by Christ ; but, however, not in order. For he neither heard the Lord, nor had been a follower of his ; but afterwards, as I said, he was a follower of Peter, who framed his teaching according to the needs (of his hearers), but not with the design of giving a connected account of the Lord's words. Thus Mark committed no error in thus writing down things as he remembered them. For he took heed to one thing : not to omit any of the things he had heard, or to set down anything falsely therein."

Here, we observe, no supernatural infallibility is ascribed to Mark—only careful recording. So again, when we read Luke's illuminating preface to his Gospel, we see that he claims no more than the necessary qualifications for writing good history—an honest intention, careful enquiry and opportunities of access to first-hand authorities as well as to already written records, which, however, did not satisfy him that nothing better and completer was needed. As we study Luke's Gospel, we see plainly that he found Mark's story among those written records: but that he treated it with a freedom which would have been impossible if he had believed in its verbal infallibility. It also becomes quite plain that both Luke and Matthew use a document (commonly nowadays known as " Q," i.e. *Quelle*, the German word for a source), which appears to have been a very early record in the main of the words of Jesus, though with some historical incidents, extending from John's Baptism down to the eve of the Passion. But, again, it is plain that Luke treats that record also with great freedom when he incorporated it, or as much of it as he had need of, among the results of his own personal enquiries from the eye-witnesses. Again, it is held (though in this book we are not arguing or laying stress upon the question) that the Fourth Gospel gives us the treasured recollections of an eye-witness, who can hardly be any other than John the Apostle, though it assumed its present shape some sixty years after the death of Jesus. But this Gospel

180 JESUS OF NAZARETH

again plainly corrects Mark and Luke (or corrects the impression which their narratives had made and still make upon their readers)—for instance, by putting on record an earlier ministry of Jesus before John was imprisoned, and also his repeated visits to Jerusalem, and once more by making it plain that the Last Supper was not the Paschal Supper of the Jews. Plainly there was so far no idea of the literal infallibility of the Gospel records. This idea was in fact adopted from the Jews who so interpreted the inspiration of their canonical Scriptures : and when the Christian Church (c. A.D. 200) formed a canon of the New Testament and placed it by the side of the Old Testament, the idea of literal infallibility passed from the latter to the former, though it was not, we gather, universally held.

But to-day we can see for ourselves that it simply is not true. The three first Gospels, though they present closely similar pictures, do not always agree in details. The proposed reconciliations of their apparent discrepancies are often forced and improbable. On such grounds we have felt constrained to give up the theory of miraculous infallibility. And it should be borne in mind that the Church never committed itself to, or made a "dogma" of, this prevalent theory. No general council dealt

ARE OUR GOSPELS TRUSTWORTHY? 181

with it, and there is nothing in the Creed concerning it, save the phrase that the Holy Spirit " spake by the prophets.". But of course without any such guaranteed infallibility, ancient historical records may give us quite good history. Thus we have very accurate knowledge of certain periods of Greek history and Roman history, or, looking farther back, of Jewish history—for instance of the reign of King David and of his character. The question is, have we such trustworthy records of Jesus' life and teaching? And there is a different question which follows—whether our documents, though not infallible, show signs of being inspired by the Spirit of Truth in a very high degree.

To-day, as I have said, a man cannot approach this enquiry without anxiety, because some of the sharpest intellects of Europe for the last two or three generations have been at work upon the four Gospels, subjecting them to a microscopic examination, to the like of which hardly any other books have ever been subjected; and the conclusions of these critics have been—by no means universally, but in great part—deeply subversive of the tradition, so that we should gather from many of them that what we have presented to us in the Gospels is rather " a Christ-myth " as it formed itself over some forty or fifty years, than the actual Jesus as he lived and taught. Now, it cannot be doubted that the critical studies of the Gospels have tended to arrive at certain very valuable results which are likely to stand firm. On the other hand, much of the criticism has been quite extravagant and transitory; and, as it is all based upon an appeal to " free thought," we must use our free thought upon it. The " superior " tone of oracular authority, in which some of the destructive critics address us, is, we shall find, quite misplaced. Different schools among these specialists, as has been already observed (see above, pp. 114–6), give us even ludicrously discrepant accounts of the real Jesus, whom they think they can discern by going behind the Gospels. Thus we gain the impression that a great deal in their method must be in a high degree arbitrary, or the results could not have been so contradictory. When we give further study to the critical literature of the more destructive kind with free minds, certain conclusions concerning it become evident.

The destructive critics have not undertaken their historical task with open minds. They profess openly, or they indicate unmistakably, certain dogmatic presuppositions of a scientific or metaphysical kind, as that what are called nature-miracles cannot have occurred : or that the idea of a personal God who can have taken definite action for the redemption of mankind, or who can have met man's efforts to discover God by a personal disclosure or divine revelation, is incredible ; or that, even if the idea of divine self-revelation is credible in some shape, yet the idea of its culminating at a definite point of history in a divine incarnation, in the person of Jesus of Nazareth alone, is out of the question. Of course if these ideas are ruled out *a priori* (that is, to start with—before the investigation begins) it is evident that the Gospel story must be rejected as it stands, even by doing violence to the evidence. For it is permeated by supernatural conceptions and a belief in miraculous occurrences. But have we the right to make such assumptions ? No doubt the materialistic philosophy of fifty years ago did give the world the impression that both the belief in " free will " in man, and the belief in " miraculous " acts of God, were ruled out by science. But this kind of dogmatic materialism has had to abandon the throne it usurped. I take Professor C. W. Hobson's *Domain of Natural Science* as a representative of the present-day spirit of science, and I will cite from this book two utterances. The first (p. 233)

184 JESUS OF NAZARETH

refers to the dogma that the appearance or consciousness of "freedom" in man must be pronounced illusory. "The assertion of this view, in its absolute form, is merely a dogma resting on an extension to a whole, of what may have been shown to be true of some parts." The second regards miracles: "It must, however, be distinctly recognized that there exists, and can exist, no *a priori* proof of the impossibility of what are called miracles. If that impossibility has sometimes been asserted by exponents of Natural Science, the assertion is merely a piece of *a priori* dogmatism quite incapable of substantiation on scientific grounds" (p. 490). I have grouped these two repudiations together, because I believe these two questions, of free will and responsibility in men and of miracles in the action of God, are at bottom one and the same question. Rational freedom in man implies that, though in general his rationality shows itself in uniformity of conduct, yet his will, enlightened by his intelligence, can under exceptional circumstances rise above routine to extraordinary action. And it is in accordance with this principle of rationality that the Supreme Reason, while its activity in nature is marked by constancy and order, yet should not be supposed to be the slave of its own law. The fact is that of recent years science has become much more modest than it used to be in respect of the place which it can claim to hold in the whole complex of human faculty for apprehending reality. Science is concerned with what can be numbered or measured or weighed, and takes no cognizance of what are called in modern parlance " values," such as beauty and goodness, which yet have as good a claim to be considered realities as sensible objects, and therefore must be equally well taken into account when we are facing the problem of the Ultimate Reality.

Again, science in many of its best representatives has recognized the fallacy of supposing that we have " explained " the higher manifestations of life, or life itself, by laying bare the lower and material constituents out of which they appear to have had their origin. The " meaning " of creation is to be found not on its lowest levels but rather in its highest. Something like a purpose in creation must be postulated and different levels recognized, the higher interpreting the lower, rather than the lower the higher. These concessions in modern scientific theory are obviously important, if the question is whether we have in Jesus Christ a new level of life making its appearance, a new relation of humanity to the Creative Spirit.

Science by its very nature must continue to be, in one sense, materialistic. Its business is with material processes alone : and this preoccupation will no doubt continue, like every form of specialization, to make those who are exclusively occupied in it disinclined to recognize other avenues to reality. But it is much less inclined than it used to be to issue dogmatic statements exclusive of the supernatural. It is much more conscious of the limitations of its knowledge.

Christianity is rooted in the conception of God as the Father—as personal. The personality of God means, not that God is to be conceived of as in the image of man, but that —while He necessarily surpasses all that we can conceive—a far *better* image of Him can be found in human personality than in merely mechanical force or animal vitality. The best image of Him, who is in Himself beyond all human definition, is to be found in what we only know as belonging to man—will and purpose and creative energy and reason and love. Such a God, our Father, has willed to create beings like to Himself as being endowed with freedom and intelligence, and sooner than extirpate their freedom has tolerated their rebellion and wilfulness over long ages, and still tolerates it ; but He has also planned to redeem mankind out of its sin and misery; and in this redemptive purpose the central moment is reached in Jesus Christ, in whom the divine power and purpose and love takes visible and tangible form in a human character. If we are to study the Gospel to any profit or with any sympathy our minds must be at least open to some such idea of God. Then we are not likely to rule out the possibility of the miraculous or extraordinary in the case of Jesus. We can at least approach the story with an open mind and give reasonable attention to its evidences. Also the idea of a self-revealing and self-communicating God will be at least accessible to us.

But before we go on to take a fresh look at these evidences, let us turn from the men of science and the metaphysicians to the historians. Some of our great historians of recent years have been devout Christians, but over a wide area this has not been so. Thus on the subject of miracles they have been disposed to tell us that they have carefully studied human testimony and have seen grounds for declaring that the records of miracles are so unsatisfactory that you can believe none of them—you can practically " rule out that whole category of supposed events." They can all be " psychologically " explained away. But have they the right to go nearly so far ? It is quite true that most records of the miraculous in history are unreliable, either through the distance of the evidence from the supposed facts, or through the excessive expectation of the miraculous in the mind of the witness to it and his obvious readiness to be deluded. But, after all, the reputed miracles of the New Testament are not like other miracles. Jesus was quite unlike other thaumaturges. He refused consistently to dazzle by marvels : and his miracles are interwoven with his teaching as in an indissoluble fabric, and have an ethical character and purpose that are all their own. The consequence is that anyone who rejects the miraculous or the supernatural *a priori*, after he has worked his will on the Gospels, can make what he pleases out of their mangled remains. Seeley is quite right when he says: " On the whole miracles play so important a part in Christ's scheme, that any theory which would represent them as due entirely to the imagination of his followers, or of a later age, destroys the credibility of the documents not partially but wholly, and leaves Christ a personage as mythical as Hercules " (p. 49). Has the historian any sort of right to say that history can present to us nothing really unique ? Can we read this story of Jesus without there dawning upon us at point after point a sense that we have here to deal with a person in whom the relation of man to God and God to man appears to be different from what is to be found in other men, even saints and prophets? Can we say *a priori* that there can be nothing unique in such a person's powers over other men and over nature?

So we will approach the evidence in a spirit of really free thought, in spite of the authority of the critics. And indeed there is a very good reason to doubt the legitimacy of the " vigour and rigour " which the more destructive of them bring their microscopic analysis to bear upon our documents. Naïve records of personal experiences all the world over, which are quite credible on the whole, are still not drawn up with such precision as to stand minute cross-questioning. Luke, for example, gives us three accounts of Saul's conversion, two of them as proceeding from Saul himself. They contain obvious differences in detail, but they all come to us from the same recorder, who is quite content to let the minute discrepancies remain. Once more, Luke gives us two accounts of the events between the resurrection and ascension of Christ which produce quite different impressions as to the space of time occupied by these events; but, again, they both come from the same recorder, who only gives greater precision to his notes of time in the second account than in the first. That is the way with naïve records in all ages. They do not admit of rigorous cross-questioning in details, but still may be both vivid and truthful. Thus we find that whereas the method of rigorous analysis has in the past been brought to bear upon classical authors with the intention of disputing genuineness and proving diversity of sources, the method seems to be ceasing to find favour. No other ancient authorities are now expected to submit to such exaggerated tests as are still being applied to the Bible documents by sceptical critics. A few years ago the man whom we may call the greatest living authority on the history of antiquity as a whole, Eduard Meyer, found it necessary to give careful investigation to the *Origin and Beginnings of Christianity*. He is a thorough-going " rationalist " and would deal with the Christian documents without any reverential prejudice. But when, after studying for a number of years the contemporary criticism of the New Testament in Germany, he produced his history, it was found to be remarkably conservative in its estimate of the documents, and full of hostile notes upon the critics, as men who have allowed their estimate of what the facts must have been to distort their judgement of the documents, and again as men who have constantly mistaken unproved hypotheses for facts. These errors he himself would avoid: and he concludes his examination of Mark's Gospel thus:

> " The conclusion we have won is of the highest importance. It is evident that for our history Jesus we have by no means to reckon merely of with representations of the second, sub-apostolic, generation, but are taken back far behind that into the midst of the first generation who personally had known him intimately (*genau*) and still preserved a lively recollection of him ; and that these old recollections lie under our eyes in manifold forms. There is no ground at all for refusing to accept these oldest traditions as historically trustworthy in all essentials, and in their chronological ordering of the history."

Thus in particular Meyer claims that we must accept as trustworthy the tradition of Papias (already quoted, p. 178), that Mark was the author of the second Gospel and that he had been the companion and interpreter (*Dolmetscher*) of Peter in his missionary journeys, so that it is obvious that " the foundation of our tradition goes back to Peter, and that Mark in a great part of his Gospel was reproducing Peter's own memories as to how things happened at the beginning, as Peter gave them to his converts." What is not due to Peter personally in Mark's Gospel, Meyer ascribes mostly ·to a document emanating from the Church at Jerusalem in its first days. Again, Meyer accepts the tradition which makes Luke, the physician and companion of St. Paul, the author of the one work divided into two parts —the third Gospel and the Acts of the Apostles; and he will have us recognize in Luke's work, "one of the most important historical works which remains to us from antiquity." Once more he accepts generally the genuineness of St. Paul's Epistles, and lays great stress on St. Paul's references to the tradition which he tells the Corinthians he had "received" and "delivered" to his converts—of which he says, "Whether it was I or they (the Twelve) so we preach and so ye believe." Meyer will not admit the legitimacy of any doubt that the "first formulated tradition" which St. Paul recites of the institution of the Eucharist and of the death, burial and resurrection of Jesus was what he received immediately on his conversion at Damascus, and in his subsequent visit to Jerusalem to question Peter; where also he found a record of the words of the Lord to which he sometimes refers as of final authority—as an end of controversy.

ARE OUR GOSPELS TRUSTWORTHY? 193

Now of course Meyer, retaining as he does his conviction that nothing supernatural or miraculous can really have occurred, has to treat these records, the genuineness of which he acknowledges, with considerable violence. All that I am laying stress on is this, that a first-rate historical authority, as far removed as possible from orthodox prejudices, demands of scholars that they should accept Mark's Gospel and Luke's Gospel and the great bulk of St. Paul's Epistles as being in respect of authorship what the tradition of the Church has always represented them as being, and we find this judgement coinciding with Adolf Harnack's earlier demand for " a return to tradition " about the New Testament documents generally.

I have myself no doubt about the validity of these conclusions, and for this reason I have been working in the earlier chapters of this volume upon the basis of Mark and Luke's Gospels. What I am seeking first of all to maintain is that, judged impartially, these writers must be admitted to have been witnesses who were at least in a position to write thoroughly good history.

2. *Mark's Gospel*

John Mark had been brought up at Jerusalem in his mother's house, which we find to be a centre of the apostolic group at the time of Peter's captivity and release in A.D. 44. We saw reason to believe that as a youth he had witnessed the capture of Jesus, and that it was probably at his father's house that the Apostles had assembled for the Last Supper, and assembled again after Jesus had left them. Before 44 he must have become thoroughly impregnated with the tradition of the Twelve about Jesus. Then he became the companion of Paul and Barnabas at Antioch and in the beginning of their first missionary journey; later, when Paul was offended by his refusal to continue with them, we find him going upon another mission alone with his cousin Barnabas, a man who almost ranked with the Twelve. Later, according to a trustworthy tradition, he became the permanent attendant upon Peter, and still later, in the last days of Peter and Paul at Rome, we find him the much loved and trusted minister to both of them. This man then had the best opportunities for becoming a faithful and trustworthy recorder of the apostolic witness. And his Gospel is remarkably reassuring. It exhibits no literary skill, but abundant evidence of faithfulness. For instance, naïve expressions which represent Jesus as needing to ask questions for information, or as exhibiting strong human

ARE OUR GOSPELS TRUSTWORTHY? 195

emotions, or the Apostles as hardened in heart—such expressions as Luke or Matthew will not reproduce, no doubt as savouring of irreverence to Jesus (e.g. iii. 5 ; iii. 21 ; vi. 3, 5, 6 ; ix. 21, 33 ; x. 14, 17 ; xiv. 33), or of disrespect to the Apostles (vi. 52 ; viii. 17)—seem to raise no scruple in Mark's mind. And there are traits in his narratives which highly favour its attribution (in the main) to Peter. Thus in Mark we find the movements of Jesus and his attendants constantly recorded with the plural pronoun "they," whereas in Matthew and Luke, repeating Mark, more frequently than not the "they" has vanished and often a "he" is substituted. What is so natural an explanation of this as that Mark is recalling the story of an eye-witness, which ran "*we* went," "*we* entered," etc., and simply translates it into the third person? (This is a delicate observation of Prof. Cuthbert Turner's, who has made St. Mark's Gospel a life-study.) And if we ask who was this eye-witness, the internal evidence strongly confirms the tradition that Peter was the man.

We must not say that all Mark's Gospel came from Peter—not perhaps the Apocalyptic discourse or the story of the Feeding of the Four Thousand, which, we have already said, shows signs of being a doublet. Nor need we suppose that Peter's memory was quite unfailing. We wonder whether the repeated prophecies attributed to Jesus of his trial, death and resurrection have not become in memory more precise and definite than they were in fact. Or we wonder whether in the story of the Gadarene demoniac, the original narrator, even if he were Peter, may not have mistaken some gesture of Jesus for a permission to the devils to enter the swine—which seems to us grotesque and unworthy. Still, the total impression made by this Gospel upon our minds seems to the present writer to be an irresistible impression of reality. Nothing can be less like a gradual production of the myth-making faculty. That would have produced something surely utterly different— something much more vulgar and cheap, like those other early products of the myth-making faculty among the Christians, the " Apocryphal Gospels." Nor can we find in Mark's Gospel any appreciable traces of later doctrinal theory remodelling the facts. The attribution to it of " Paulinism " is quite unwarranted. Surely it is a healthy modern instinct which had lifted into the place of supreme importance this Gospel, so long despised by comparison with Matthew and Luke. True it is that in this brief record Jesus, while truly man is yet surely something more : and is endowed with miraculous powers over nature as well as over men. But the miraculous powers are all of a piece with what seems to be a more than barely human personality and authority. Is it conceivable that either myth-making could have produced such a figure, or that there was in the earliest Christian Church any single imagination which could have invented it?

3. *St. Luke*

Let us pass from St. Mark to St. Luke. The closest examination by the philologists has verified the ascription of the Acts and the Gospel to the same author, and there is no assignable author so probable as the one designated by constant tradition—Luke " the beloved physician " and companion of St. Paul. His preface tells us of his serious intention to reproduce in his Gospel the record of " the eye-witnesses and ministers of the word." He had good opportunities of gathering materials. He was with St. Paul at Cæsarea " many days," lodging with Philip, one of " the Seven " : he was taken up to Jerusalem by an " original disciple," and was there for a short period during which St. Paul was arrested. Then he was with him at Cæsarea during his two years captivity (A.D. 56–8). It is probable on internal evidence that, while at Cæsarea, he composed a "first draft" of his Gospel, combining the document Q with the information he had gathered independently, and only at a later date at Rome, when he was in Mark's company, became acquainted with the substance of his Gospel, and proceeded to incorporate as much of it as he wanted, or had room for, in his own.

As has been said, there are more signs in Luke than in Mark of what may be called theological scruple. He seems to have found some of Mark's naïve expressions irreverent towards Jesus or disrespectful towards the apostles, and to have softened or omitted them. He omits Jesus' affirmation of ignorance as to the time of the end (Mark xiii. 32), though it would have served his purpose—for he plainly desires to counteract a current tendency to ascribe to Jesus the assurance that it would come immediately. He omits also the awful question asked on the Cross, "My God, my God, why?" On the other hand, certain features in the teaching of Jesus are plainly specially dear to his heart—his high regard for women, his hatred of wealth and arrogance, his love of poverty and humility and mercy. And it must be said that all that we owe to Luke only in his Gospel bears strongly the impress of authenticity, and belongs to what the best conscience of man has most readily assimilated.

There are two reasonable views as to the date of Luke's Gospel—that it was composed about A.D. 62 or about 75—but, in either case, Luke must be judged a competent author whose opportunities of gathering first-hand information were very good.

On these grounds we have based our account of Jesus' life on the Gospels of Mark and Luke in the main. We must be content to give only a brief account of the two other evangelists.

4. *St. Matthew, St. John, and St. Paul*

The same Papias who gives us the account of Mark's Gospel, tells us also in another fragment of his book, which has survived, that " Matthew compiled the oracles in the Hebrew speech, and each man interpreted them according to his ability." It may well be that this compilation by Matthew was the document (Q) consisting mainly of discourses, but with a certain amount of incident, which underlies both St. Luke's Gospel and our " Gospel according to St. Matthew." But our Gospel is certainly not a translation from a Hebrew or

Aramaic original. It must, we conclude, be the work of some unknown Palestinian editor, who combined St. Matthew's "oracles" with St. Mark's Gospel and introduced other matter independent of either; and there are features in the independent portions of our "St. Matthew" which reasonable critics are unwilling to accept as historical. Thus, though it has ranked throughout Church history as the premier Gospel, it has seemed better to appeal in this little volume mainly to the two others which contain the greater parts of its substance. After all, the general impression given us by " St. Matthew " of the person and teaching of Jesus is so much the same as that given by the others, as that it requires careful reading to perceive any difference.

The Fourth Gospel is considerably later than the other three—commonly called the Synoptic Gospels. It may be dated about A.D. 90. We may agree with Eduard Meyer that the author certainly intended to represent himself as John the Apostle. "That," Meyer says, " was the mask he assumed." But the present writer believes that the evidence on the whole points strongly to the conclusion that he was truly the Son of Zebedee writing in extreme old age at Ephesus with the help of some of his disciples

ARE OUR GOSPELS TRUSTWORTHY ? 201

as editors: and that the substance of his Gospel (apart from the Introduction) was probably the long familiar substance of his teaching. There is a growing recognition among sensible critics that at least the whole book is thoroughly Hebraic and not Hellenistic, and that it reproduces a genuine memory of an intimate disciple well acquainted with Jerusalem. We have already in our account of the life of Jesus recognized the importance at point after point of the historical information it supplies. We may also agree cordially with Professor Leonard Hodgson (in his recent work *And Was Made Man*, chap. viii) that the point of view of Jesus in the discourses of this Gospel is not so different as is commonly supposed from that of the Jesus of the Synoptists. We may think that the mistake of the critics is that they read the Introduction into the substance of the Gospel—whereas the introduction was probably written after the rest of the Gospel, partly as a means of commending the record to the consideration of the Hellenistic world in which the aged Apostle now lived. We may also recognize that, so far as concerns the discourses in the Fourth Gospel, there is no line of demarcation indicated between the utterances of Jesus himself and the comment or meditation thereon of the author, while still holding that each discourse represents truly something actually said by Jesus. But though all these considerations are true, it still remains the case that the Fourth Gospel is supplementary. It presupposes the Gospel of Mark, and surely also that of Luke. If it supplies their deficiencies, it thereby affirms their contents in general. It justifies us in taking the first written Gospels for first consideration and basing our point of view upon them; and the unsettled state of the contemporary mind—even in orthodox circles—about the Fourth Gospel, makes this course prudent. We must return to it, however, when we are speaking of the Gospel of Jesus as it went out into the world.

Something must be added about St. Paul. It is very important to study the passages in 1 Corinthians xi. 23–34, xv. 1–11, and vii. 10. In the first two he is telling his converts what he "delivered" to them as a formulated statement when he first came among them in A.D. 50, which he tells them was what he "received"— that is, at his conversion in Damascus or in his subsequent visit to Jerusalem (? A.D. 37) when he went there to make enquiries of Peter; of which he further says, that it was common to him with the Twelve—" whether it were I

ARE OUR GOSPELS TRUSTWORTHY? 203

or they, so we preach and so ye believe." Anyone who examines these passages will see that the Christ of "the tradition" from the first years after the crucifixion was someone quite as certainly elevated above the level of common humanity, and miraculous, as the Christ of St. Mark and St. Luke's Gospel thirty years later. It also appears in the third passage, and elsewhere in St. Paul's Epistles, that there was a collection of Christ's sayings already in existence to which he could appeal to as of final authority, and which may very well have been already written.

5. *A Reasonable Conclusion*

Now we return to the questions we asked at the beginning of this chapter. We must ask for the admission that the authors St. Mark and St. Luke were persons who were in a position to write thoroughly good history and to fulfil the kind of intention expressed in St. Luke's admirable Preface to his Gospel. We want the further admissions that we are not, as human beings, rationally justified in excluding *a priori* from our minds the evidence of the miraculous and the supernatural: and that, supposing supernatural manifestations are rationally conceivable in any position in history, they are so in the case of Jesus Christ, if it appears

204 JESUS OF NAZARETH

that he occupies the central position in a divine purpose of redemption for mankind. The miracles in the picture of Christ are not, as in the case of thaumaturgic characters generally, detachable from the main history. They are inextricably interwoven into the character and the personality, as it is presented to us—so much so that, if we reject the miraculous element, we have hardly anything certain remaining.

Once more, the person presented to us by the Gospels is not in the least like the products of the myth-making faculty, as we see it in history. The Buddha-myth is fairly easily separable from the historic man Siddhartha Gautama. It is the sort of myth that we should have expected to grow up. And it is an excrescence upon the historical figure, which it indeed conceals but does not obliterate. The same is not at all true of the Person in the Gospels. That Figure is indeed life-like and self-consistent in the highest degree. It has not to any appreciable extent the vulgarizing characteristics of the myth. Moreover it quite overtops any rational estimate of what the imagination of any individual or group could have conceived or executed. We must recognize that the great masters of imagination have not attempted to depict the sinless man, and have failed to depict even the male saint, without making him as colourless as Tennyson's King Arthur, or a prig, like Sir Charles Grandison, or a half-witted eccentric—however lovable—like Don Quixote. Their power seems constantly to demand the mixed character to work upon. But Jesus is full of colour—of a rich humanity —combining a profound humility with tremendous authority, and a holy indignation with the tenderest love: and yet withal self-consistent, and the supreme model of perfection.

The sum of our answer is this: historical evidence never is, or can be, demonstrative evidence, such as can put an absolute constraint upon the wills of men or their reasons. There always remains room for faith or, on the other hand, the opportunity to escape conviction. The final determination between faith and unfaith in the case of Jesus, certainly rests upon the consideration—Do I or do I not find room in my mind for the idea of God as the Creator and the Redeemer of men in general and of myself in particular, who comes near to mankind and to me at last in a human character— in Jesus of Nazareth? If we can find in our mind no room for this Divine Saviour, we shall find means no doubt to dispose of the evidence. But if we find room for the idea, we shall also find the evidence very cogent—enough, or more than enough, to make the self-committal of faith the reasonable reaction.

There are two points—one concerning the words and one concerning the works of Jesus —on which something must still be said.

1. When we were considering the form of the teaching of Jesus (above, p. 93) we observed that the poetical parallelism in which it is so often expressed would make it singularly easy to remember, even to the very words. The same is true, though not probably to the same extent, of the story-telling in the parables. So it is that, as we read the words of Jesus in the Synoptic Gospels, and in many parts of St. John, we feel that he must have said precisely that. And if we try to imagine the state of mind of the Twelve, after Jesus had passed away, filled with an adoring love of their Master, and also with a deep sense of shame at their long continued " hardness " or " slowness " of heart in their attitude to the Great Teacher while he was with them, we cannot doubt that from the first they must have been deeply occupied in recalling, and one would suppose in writing down and comparing, their personal memories of his words in the context of his actions and his movements. In this connection it is worth

ARE OUR GOSPELS TRUSTWORTHY ? 207

while recalling Mr. Bruce Glasier's experience when he was writing his Memoir of William Morris, as much as twenty-five years after his death : " I have found that my memory is, on many occasions, subject to what seems to be a sort of ' illumination ' or ' inspiration.' Thus when I have fixed my mind on one, say, of the incidents recalled in these chapters, the scene has begun to unfold itself, perhaps slowly at first, but afterwards rapidly and clearly. Meditating upon it for a time, I have lifted my pen and begun to write. Then to my surprise the conversations, long buried or hidden somewhere in my memory, have come back to me sometimes with the greatest fullness, word for word, as we say. Nay, not only the words, but the tones, the pauses and the gestures of the speaker."[1] We cannot suppose that the writing down of the Master's words in the circle of the Apostles, in the form in which they were found in the foundation-document which we call Q, was delayed nearly so many years as is here described. But surely the reappearance of former incidents and conversations in the conscious memory out of the subconscious is an experience which is fairly com-

[1] Quoted in D. C. Somervell's *Short History of Our Religion*, p. 108.

mon, especially under the stress of strong feeling. Thus Mr. Glasier's experience helps us to imagine the process by which Christ's words were preserved for succeeding generations by the effort of individual Apostles, checked by the common memory, during the years when they were all together at Jerusalem.

But some of us would not feel satisfied even by all these considerations taken together. They would be enough to give us assurance about the historicity of the Gospels in a general sense. But there is something more than this which we seem to find in the Gospels—the more certainly the longer we study them; that "something more" is not indeed infallibility in detail, but it is a high degree of accuracy. We often feel as we study the acts and words, as described in our documents, that we are present at the very scenes and listening to the very words: and, in justification of this feeling, we reflect that, if it was truly the Father who sent Jesus into the world, that men in the words and works of the messenger might really hear and see Him who sent him, it is difficult to imagine that He should then have suffered the message to be effaced or seriously misrepresented at the very moment of its delivery to the wider world. Then we recall the promise to the

Twelve, recorded in St. John : " the Paraclete, even the Holy Spirit, whom the Father will send in my name, he shall . . . bring to your remembrance all that I said unto you." Inspiration does not, it appears, convey infallibility in detail : but it gives a guarantee that the message is truly delivered. We must suffer our conception of inspiration to be moulded by the facts as they appear. But the facts assuredly support the belief that the men who first conveyed to the world the story of Christ were—not infallible—but inspired in a high degree by the Spirit of Truth.

2. As to the miracles, it is nowadays often said that, whereas our forefathers accepted the miracles as proofs of the doctrine, we now in our generation find them an obstacle rather than a proof, and would sooner be without them. But this is surely the language of unregulated reaction. That the miracles have been found in the past to be proofs convincing to men's minds is certainly true ; and it is also true that much too much stress, or a too isolated stress, has often been laid upon them, especially in the period of theology in our own country of which Paley is commonly taken as the representative. In the New Testament miracles, as such, are not regarded as proofs of anything more than superhuman agency, which may be

evil as well as good. We hear a good deal about the possibility of diabolic miracles. The merely marvellous is by no means to carry conviction as to the truth of the message which accompanies it, nor the absence of miracle to discredit the message. "John," we read, "did no sign (or miracle), but all things whatsoever John spoke of this man were true." Nevertheless we cannot doubt how large a part in generating the ultimate conviction of the first disciples about Jesus was played by his "works" or "powers," and it is impossible to imagine that the Gospel would ever have gone out into the world if the experience of Jesus had ended for the disciples in his death upon the cross. Undoubtedly "the Gospel" was based upon the experience of the empty tomb and the appearances of the risen Master. That that was so at the beginning would not be doubted even by those who in various degrees hold that group of experiences to have been illusory. But they would contend that this need not be so now. For us the illusion of miracles may be dispelled and the faith still remain. Such a hypothesis seems to me to be most improbable in any general sense. The main obstacle to faith in the good tidings of God, which is associated with the name of

Jesus, is the obstinate appearance of indifference to moral considerations in material Nature. The faith postulates an infinite care for individuals in the supreme Creator and Governor of the world of Nature. Yet facts so constantly seem to contradict this faith. Now we can believe that faith needs a vigorous probation. It is a capacity for "endurance, as seeing him who is invisible." But that at the central moment of the divine self-disclosure, postulated by the Gospels, Jesus, the very representative and embodiment of God, should have been suffered to fail, and been done to death and passed into dissolution, unvindicated by the God of nature, or vindicated only to the credulous imagination of his followers by illusory appearances, would be a strain on human faith much too great for it. Men might continue to believe in Jesus as " one of the prophets," but, if the God who is the supreme power in nature did not really vindicate him by the resurrection from the dead, neither faith in the Gospel, nor faith in the Gospels, in any real sense, would long continue. The belief in the resurrection as a physical fact must be taken to be part of the fundamental faith that there is in the universe, material and spiritual, only one lordship, and that the God, who is justice and love, is the only Lord.

CHAPTER VI

THE RISEN JESUS AND THE FAITH OF THE APOSTLES

AN intelligent stranger who had been living in Palestine during the public career of Jesus, who had taken a sympathetic interest in him and his movement, and had even come half-way to believing in him, would certainly on the night of the Crucifixion have felt that he had been witness of an unmitigated tragedy. So far as he had come towards believing in the divine mission of Jesus, it would have seemed to him that (in the words of the Psalmist) "the kings of the earth had stood up, and the rulers had taken counsel together, against the Lord and against his anointed, saying, 'Let us break their bonds asunder, and cast away their cords from us'"—and that their revolt had been successful. So it must have seemed to the disheartened Twelve—"We thought it should have been he which should redeem Israel"—but now our hopes have

JESUS AND THE APOSTLES 213

been buried with him in the tomb. We must now seek to understand how this seeming failure was converted into victory, and the shame of the Cross into glory.

1. *The Records of the Resurrection*

The earliest written record that we have of the transformation is that given in St. Paul's First Epistle to the Corinthians (cap. 15), a passage already referred to, in which he recites over again to his Corinthian converts the definite form of words which he delivered to them when he first came among them in A.D. 50, but which he " received "—he must mean, after his conversion at Damascus in 34 or 35 and at Jerusalem in 37 or 38. Probably, even then, the substance of this record was not news to this brilliant " young man." He had been a strenuous persecutor of the Christians in the years before his conversion: and so able and argumentative a man as he was would have been fairly sure to have made himself acquainted with all there was to be known by one outside their circle about this " Jesus, who was dead," but whom the disciples " affirmed to be alive."

We had better have the words of St. Paul's letter in full under our eyes:

"I make known unto you, brethren," he writes, "the Gospel which I preached unto you, which also ye received, wherein also ye stand, by which also ye are being saved, if ye hold fast in what words (or 'in what sense') I preached the Gospel to you—except ye believed in vain. For I delivered unto you first of all, what also I received, that Christ died on behalf of our sins according to the scriptures, and that he was buried, and that he has been raised up on the third day according to the scriptures, and that he appeared to Cephas, then to the Twelve; then he appeared to about five hundred brethren at once, of whom the greater part remain until now, but some are fallen asleep; then he appeared to James; then to all the Apostles; and last of all, as unto one born out of due time, he appeared to me also. . . . Whether then it be I or they, so we preach and so ye believed."

Efforts have been made in various ways, by an over-meticulous examination of St. Paul's words, to weaken the force of his statement. So much importance attaches to it that we had better consider these suggestions.

First, it has been urged that a certain change in grammatical structure and phraseology between the earlier part of his statement and the later indicates that the original official formula ended with the words "then to the Twelve": and that the words which followed—"then he appeared, etc."—belong to a later expansion of the original formula, which has been ascribed

JESUS AND THE APOSTLES 215

to the community at Jerusalem, and not to the Twelve. This is not very convincing nor very important. St. Paul certainly appears to mean that he " received " the whole record—except of course what concerns his own conversion. Next, with a view to disparaging the records of the Appearances in the Gospels, it has been urged that St. Paul's own conversion was due to an appearance in the heavens of the glorified Christ, and that as he puts this in line with the earlier appearances, he must have supposed that they too were celestial visions. But this is surely a bad argument, as St. Paul reckons the appearance to himself as abnormal, such as could be compared to an irregular birth. Lastly, it has been said that St. Paul in the later part of the chapter is contemplating a " resurrection " of dead men which is compatible with their mortal bodies having " seen corruption " in the earth, and that his idea of Christ's resurrection need not have involved anything different in his case. He does not, it is added, mention the empty tomb.

To meet this suggestion it is necessary briefly to recall the point of St. Paul's whole argument. It is to reassure some of the Corinthians, who do not appear to have doubted the fact of the resurrection of Christ, but were perplexed, like the Thessalonians, by the death of some of their fellow converts, whom they had hoped would all have survived to the glorious day of Christ's return, and for whom, now dead and decaying in the tomb, they saw no hope of resurrection. St. Paul then seeks to reassure them, first by re-emphasizing as an indisputable fact the resurrection of Christ, without which he vehemently protests there could be no Gospel and the Christian hope would have no ground to rest on : and Christ's resurrection he certainly conceives as a concrete event—something that happened on the third day, and happened to that in which Christ died and was buried, that is his earthly body. That St. Paul's idea of this resurrection was that of a transformation of the mortal and corruptible body into the immortal, incorruptible and glorious body, is supported by what follows later, when he contemplates a similar change, only more rapid—" in a moment, in the twinkling of an eye "—as destined to occur in the case of those who should survive to the day of Christ's return, among whom he still hopes that he himself will be. In a moment, he imagines, they are to suffer a change of their " body of humiliation " into their " body of glory." For those who are already dead and buried St. Paul conceives a different mode of transition. For

JESUS AND THE APOSTLES 217

them, too, the mortal and corruptible body is to be exchanged for one immortal, incorruptible and spiritual. But he clearly does not contemplate any re-collection of the material particles of their dead bodies. They will on the day of resurrection be reclothed, by an act of God, in the spiritual body, which will be in some sort of continuity (which St. Paul does not clearly explain) with their old body, but which he speaks of as new and different. Thus there certainly is, as St. Paul conceives it, a kind of resurrection which is compatible with the decay of the former body: but that he did not so interpret Christ's resurrection is shown by his definite language about it, and by the picture which is in his mind of the instantaneous " change " which he anticipates for those who survive till the end.

It is only, however, with the resurrection of Christ that we are now concerned. No fair argument can throw doubt upon the certainty which St. Paul attached to the resurrection of Christ on the third day from the dead in the same body in which he died and was buried, only now transformed into the spiritual and incorruptible state, as to which something more must be said. The " official " character of the formula which St. Paul recites, as something common to him and to the other Apostles, explains, we may suppose, why only appearances to the official witnesses—the Twelve and James, the Lord's brother, who very early was ranked with them—should have been recorded, with, in addition, the appearance to quite a crowd of persons, which in all probability could only have been in Galilee. The meticulous cross-questioning of the plain language of St. Paul by those whò have sought to dissolve its force does not really deserve the name of historical criticism.

But what is St. Paul's idea of the "spiritual," "incorruptible," or "glorious" body of the resurrection, whether in Christ's case or ours? He puts it in contrast to the body of "flesh and blood," which is corruptible, and which he calls elsewhere "the body of our humiliation." Neither here nor elsewhere does he put "spiritual" into contrast with "material." St. Paul in fact never uses the word "matter" or "material" in our sense—or perhaps it should be said, in the sense we ued to attach to it, before the physicists had so refined our idea of matter, in its ultimate elements, as to cause it entirely to lose its former grossness. He means by "spiritual" what is controlled by spirit. The "spiritual" body,

JESUS AND THE APOSTLES 219

therefore, is a body which is no longer an impediment to the spirit, or a clog upon it, but its pure and unhindered expression, absolutely subservient to its will. As we shall see, the same idea of the body in which Christ rose underlies the narratives of the appearances in the Gospel.

The other chief foundation-stone on which the reality of Christ's resurrection reposes is the total transformation of the minds of the Twelve within the period of a few weeks. No reasonable criticism can explain away the picture we are given of the Apostles' " hardened " state of mind in face of the idea of the Cross before the Crucifixion, and the mental gloom into which that event plunged them—so that the first reports of the resurrection " seemed to them but idle tales "; nor can any reasonable criticism lead us to doubt the picture we are given of them a few weeks later—confident, radiant men, ready to face what would have seemed to be the impossible task of converting a hostile world to the new Gospel—ready for anything, including death itself. Such they are, because they feel their feet resting on an unshakable rock of experience, the experience of Christ risen and alive, which had given a wholly new colour to their minds and orientation to their lives. Such a complete mental change in this whole body of unimaginative men—really "slow of heart"—must have had some very solid cause. They would not have been forced round so sharp a corner to such a new outlook on life except by some very definite force. And there is not any reasonable ground for doubting that they would have ascribed their conversion to the fact that they had repeatedly seen their Lord.

Now we must apply our minds to the stories of Jesus after his resurrection in the Four Gospels. St. Mark, our first recorder, whose trustworthiness we have learned to value, gives us, like all the others, the story of the women coming to the tomb on the Sunday morning; and tells us how they found it open and empty, save that they see "a young man arrayed in a white robe" who tells them that Christ is risen and sends them to carry to Peter and the other disciples the direction to go into Galilee where, according to his former word, they are to see him. Then they are described as fleeing, trembling and astonished, not daring to tell anyone. There the original Gospel of St. Mark ends abruptly—(Mark xvi. 8)—the manuscript evidence leaves us no doubt of this. The other verses (9 to 20) are a later supplement—the original Gospel having never been

JESUS AND THE APOSTLES 221

finished, or (more probably) having had its conclusion torn off by some mischance before it was copied. The story of the women and the empty tomb, and the angelic messenger or messengers, appears also, though with minor discrepancies, in Luke, and Matthew and John. John concentrates on the experience of one only of the women, Mary of Magdala; but the single word " we " in her speech to the disciples (John xx. 2) shows her as one of a band. The discrepancies of detail are surely such as ought only to cause in our minds a sense of satisfaction that no harmonizing instinct was allowed to obliterate them. They are only such as *ought* to occur in any testimonies not manipulated by art in the interests of rigid consistency. The first Gospel—St. Matthew—normally follows Mark, and we are naturally inclined to suppose that (apart from the story about the guard, which is commonly taken for later legend) the account of the appearance in Galilee rests on Mark's unmutilated narrative. The stories of the appearances should be read in the Gospels: but there are certain considerations bearing upon these narratives to which consideration ought to be given.

1. Anyone who reads with simple attention

the most detailed of the stories—the story of the walk to Emmaus and all the stories in John xx. and xxi.—will be struck with their extraordinarily vivid and life-like character. This could not be said of all of them—not certainly of the conclusion of St. Matthew: but it is surely true of most of them. If a man is able to admit the possibility of resurrection from the dead as a phase in the evolution of human life, and further is impressed with the sense of reality about the records of the life of Jesus down to the Crucifixion, it is surely the case that he must find these stories of the appearances of the risen Jesus to his intimate friends in a high degree self-evidencing and convincing. There is no realm in which the mere imagination of men would have been more likely to produce vulgar and "cheap" results than in the construction of stories of the reappearances of Jesus. But this story of the walk to Emmaus, or of Peter and John's visit to the tomb, or of the recovery of the faith of Thomas! or that of the Apostles again turned to fishermen on the Lake of Galilee, and of Peter's restoration to his old office! Can one find any justification in the literature of the first century, let alone the literature of Palestine, for supposing that there could have

JESUS AND THE APOSTLES 223

been any individual whose imagination was capable of constructing such stories ? or is it reasonable to suppose that the myth-making faculty could have done any such work in the mind of any group or crowd ?

It will be useful to put in contrast to these stories an account of the resurrection of Jesus which is a really "mythical" development or an effort of individual imagination. It comes from a second-century apocryphal "Gospel of Peter."

"Now in the night whereon the Lord's Day dawned, as the soldiers were keeping guard two by two in every watch, there came a great sound in the heaven, and they saw the heavens opened and two men descend thence, shining with a great light, and drawing near unto the sepulchre. And that stone which had been set on the door rolled away of itself and went back to the side, and the sepulchre was opened, and both of the young men entered it. When therefore these soldiers saw that, they waked up the centurion and the elders (for they also were there keeping watch); and while they were yet telling them the things which they had seen, they saw again three men come out of the sepulchre, and two of them sustaining the other and a cross following after them. And of the two they saw that their heads reached unto heaven, but of him that was led by them, that it overpassed the heavens. And they heard a voice out of the heavens saying : Hast thou preached unto them that sleep ? And an answer was heard from the cross, saying : Yea."

224 JESUS OF NAZARETH

Here we have a not unfavourable specimen of what the myth-making imagination, working on the story of the guard which is found in Matthew, and partly influenced by the common interest in the visit of Jesus to the abode of the dead, could produce. Is it not in remarkable contrast to the narratives in Luke and John just referred to ?

2. The only arresting discrepancy in the narratives of the appearances is that whereas Mark points to, and Matthew relates, only an appearance in Galilee, Luke relates only appearances in Jerusalem, and seems to be ignorant of any others, for he has altered the reference to Galilee, which in his narrative appears quite changed from its original significance. May not the explanation of this discrepancy be simple ? Thus : Jesus did intend his disciples to go at once to Galilee, and welcome him there in the old centre of his ministry ; but his intention was, as so often, baffled by their slowness of heart. They had to be convinced on the spot, in Jerusalem, before they would move. This work of conviction, John tells us, took eight days to accomplish : but that, if Luke's reckoning of days in the Acts is right, leaves thirty days before the final disappearance of Jesus : quite enough to allow time for the

JESUS AND THE APOSTLES 225

visit to Galilee (three or four days' walk) and return. We must suppose, however, that Luke, at any rate when he composed his Gospel, did not know of any visit to Galilee. Galilee in fact faded very soon out of any present importance in the mental horizon of the early Church. By the time Luke was in Palestine making his enquiries, it had ceased to count. The Syrian Antioch and Damascus to the north, the towns on the coast, Tyre and Joppa and Cæsarea, and Samaria also, are mentioned as Christian centres, but there is only one mention of Galilee. Luke, we may suppose, hearing nothing about it, accommodates the phrase about Galilee, in the Lord's message to the disciples, to his ignorance. But, as we observed, St. Paul's brief list of appearances seems to imply an appearance in Galilee to the " 400 brethren," and the story in the last chapter of St. John reads like a vivid memory.

3. It is to be remarked that the accounts of the Appearances in all four Gospels presuppose that the Resurrection of Jesus was not a mere physical resuscitation; they involve the idea, which we saw to be clearly in St. Paul's mind, of a transition from a body of " flesh and blood " to a " spiritual body." After the Resurrection Jesus does not appear in any of the accounts

to be living here or there, so that the disciples could find him: he has passed into a higher mode of being, of which mankind had had no previous experience, out of which he "manifested" himself in one form or another form, as suited his purpose. (The sceptical questions raised even by serious men about the clothes of the risen Jesus, and how he could have put them on in the tomb, are wholly irrelevant: the clothes were no doubt simply part of the particular "manifestation.") The precise account of the state in which the grave-clothes were found by Peter and John—the linen, which had wrapped the body, lying flat on the ledge, and the napkin which had wrapped the head fallen in folds apart—must mean that the body had passed out of them and left them to collapse: the rolling away of the stone was not required to allow Jesus to depart, but was done to show that the tomb was empty: he appeared in the closed room to the disciples, shut doors being no obstacles to him: he could "materialize," even to the extent of eating with the disciples, but it was a "manifestation" for the purpose of producing conviction, not, we should gather, a sign of any physical need. These recorded experiences appear to have formed the basis of St. Paul's vague but impressive

JESUS AND THE APOSTLES 227

idea of a "spiritual body," that is a body which is no longer the master of the spirit, in any sense, but simply the expression of its will —"material," if you will, but quite raised above the conditions of materiality as we know them in common life.

4. The angelic appearances at the tomb and at the Ascension have been a stumbling-block to many. We may notice that an "angel" in the Bible is not a creature with wings, such as the artists have familiarized us with, but simply a manlike form which is only discerned not to be a man by later indications. This is what we commonly understand as an "apparition." All ghosts or apparitions were dismissed as fiction by our Victorian forefathers, but to-day if one were to cross-question any company, one would probably find only a minority completely sceptical. Certainly the disciples of Jesus believed that angels existed and could appear to men, and we have no reason to doubt that at the tomb and at the Ascension they believed that they had seen angels and had received information from them. On the other hand the evidence for the objective reality of these appearances is not nearly so strong as in the case of the recorded appearances of the risen Jesus; and the question is not of vital importance.

5. The last manifestation recorded of Jesus on the earth was the Ascension, the story of which is only given in any detail at the beginning of the Acts, though the New Testament generally refers to it as a particular event. It is commonly made an objection to the historicity of this account that it presupposes the ignorant idea of a heaven above the round vault of the sky into which Jesus passes to sit on the right hand of the Father. But though such a crude idea—like the idea that the "resurrection of the dead" would involve the re-collection of the material particles of the decayed body—possessed the minds of the multitude and of many of their teachers in the early centuries of our era, the wiser minds saw its falsity. The pugnacious scholar Jerome (c. A.D. 400) ridicules it as a striking instance of the "vain talking" which did the Church so much mischief with the educated world. The Alexandrian scholars repudiated it. All the Christian teachers knew that "the right hand of the Father" was only a metaphor. Though Paul once uses the Jewish phrase "the third heaven," yet when he talks about "heaven," or "the heavenlies," where "Christ is seated" as a sphere in which Christians are already living ("our conversation is in heaven"), he shows that he knew

JESUS AND THE APOSTLES 229

heaven was not a district beyond the stars. Heaven was, to his mind, one of those realities of which he speaks, of which at present we can have no adequate " knowledge," but can only receive some dim reflection as in a mirror, or a riddle. The same is true of the author of the Epistle to the Hebrews, who freely uses spacial metaphors about Christ's ascent into heaven, but also tells his fellow Christians that they have already " come " into actual experience of the realities of heaven.

There is thus no real excuse for saying that the Ascension of Jesus has no meaning for those who have ceased to believe in the " three-storied universe." The Ascension was a real objective " manifestation " of Jesus mounting and received up into the cloud of the divine presence; it was quite of a kind with the other " manifestations "; and it symbolized, under the figure of a corporal ascension, what still to-day we can only express under spacial metaphors, that Jesus passed into " the highest," the sphere of the Divine Glory, the sphere which is one day to irradiate and transform all this lower world; and that thenceforth he was " sitting at God's right hand "—which means that the divine sovereignty of the universe belongs, still in complete dependence upon the Father, to one who has shared our human experiences and is for ever very man.

To Christians generally, down the generations, and to many of us to-day, the idea of the resurrection of Christ, and the narratives connected with the event, have presented, and present, no difficulty. They have understood what St. Peter meant, when he said that it was "not possible that Jesus should have been holden of death." His crucifixion and all that it meant had seemed to postulate that, if God is God, He should vindicate His Christ. It would have been the absence of any such vindication, as visible and actual as the apparent defeat, which would have created an insurmountable difficulty. On the other hand, there are those whose minds are closed to any suggestion or evidence of the supernatural; and historical evidence is never demonstrative on any particular point. But in between these two groups there are many with less determined prejudices. From time to time at least they "feel through all their earthly dress bright shoots of everlastingness": they do not find it easy to "naturalize" Jesus: they are not indisposed to the idea of divine redemption, and they understand what belief in the Resurrection would mean in practical life. Such

JESUS AND THE APOSTLES 231

people, and they are many, surely must own, if they give a candid consideration to the evidences, that they are very impressive, and that the narratives are very unlike the probable products either of the myth-making faculty, or of the imagination of any individuals such as we can with probability suppose the early Church to have contained.

2. *The Consequent Idea of Jesus, the Christ*

We have been occupied with the question of fact and how the fact came to be believed; but we must go on to consider the consequences of belief in the fact, as they appeared first in the thought and life of the Twelve. The mighty event, which seemed to them to have been almost forced upon their attention, transformed their whole mind and outlook. God had vindicated Jesus and exalted him as the Christ to the throne of the world. This thought flooded their minds and restored, or more than restored, all their old confidence in Jesus. After a few days they passed through a new experience which their Master had taught them to expect—they found themselves possessed by the Spirit, the Spirit of God and of Jesus, to inspire and enable them to carry his Gospel to the world. Their old experiences of him before his death upon the cross were only a prelude. "The things that Jesus then began both to do and to teach" he was to go on doing and teaching in the larger world through them and those whom he would call. The life of Jesus was not over; his activity had only just begun. This is the impression which we get in the early chapters of the Acts. It is Jesus the Christ, risen and exalted, Jesus, Lord of all, Jesus to come again as the judge of quick and dead, which is the central figure. This gives the Apostles their sublime courage and enthusiasm and wins such sweeping successes.

But we can readily imagine the sympathetic observer from outside, whom we supposed to be upon the scene immediately after the crucifixion, being now thrown into a new perplexity. Are these Jews, he would have said, who all over the world and under all temptations have been such strenuous and fanatical monotheists, now themselves on the way to deify a man? It might have looked like it to such an observer; and in fact they were *worshipping* Jesus—for to " call upon his name " or " invoke his name " we find given as the very mark of a Christian. We find Stephen at his martyrdom invoking Jesus, as Jesus

JESUS AND THE APOSTLES 233

himself invoked the Father—"lay not this sin to their charge," "receive my spirit." A good many modern authors have, in fact, supposed that the first theology of the new movement was what is called *adoptionism*, which is only another name for the deification of the man Jesus. But this is surely a mistake. Adoptionism or deification implies that men have considered and adopted a theory. That was just what, as far as our evidence goes, the apostles had not done. Their minds were simply full of the fact that the man Jesus, whom they had known of old and seen pass into the dark valley of failure and death, had been raised from the dead and glorified as the Christ in the heavens. They worshipped him indeed: but they do not appear to have begun to form any theory about the relation of Jesus to God His Father. They were not however on their way to Adoptionism. And the man who was to light them on their way was the man who passed so suddenly from the persecution of Christians to the worship of Christ—whose Hebrew name was Saul and his Latin name Paul. It is surely not without meaning that when in the Acts we first hear Jesus called " Son of God " it is from the mouth of the just baptized Saul—" Straightway in the synagogue he proclaimed Jesus, that he is the Son of God." The Messiah as such might no doubt be called Son of God, but it was as Messiah and something more that St. Paul called him by that name.

It is noticeable that St. Paul after his conversion passed through long periods of leisure from distraction and work—first the years in Arabia, and then, after his brief visit to Jerusalem, the years, which seem to have been mainly years of retirement, at his home at Tarsus. When we come to read his Epistles written during his later years of stress and strain, we find his interpretation of the person of Christ quite consistent. This, we imagine, was the result of prolonged meditation. He interprets it on the principle of the Incarnation. Jesus is the " only Son " of God. He belongs to His being before ever the world was, for it was through him that all things were made, whether things in heaven or things on earth. He is immanent in all creation as its principle of coherence, and he is the final end of all things. It was as a consummate act of self-sacrifice that, in the fullness of the time, he, who preexisted in the nature of God, but thought not equality with God a prize to be clutched at, emptied himself, or impoverished himself, for love of us, and taking the servile nature of man, was born of a woman, under the law, man like other men, and humbled himself, becoming obedient even to death, the death of the cross. Thus it was that God could so highly exalt the man Jesus and give him the Supreme Name, so that at the name of Jesus every knee should bow, and that he should sit on high, above every kind of authority and power in the universe, and that every tongue should confess him Lord. This exaltation of the Man was possible because essentially and originally he belongs to the Divine Being. Only once does St. Paul fairly certainly call him by the name of God. But he attributes to him constantly divine functions and co-ordinates his activities with the activities of the Father, preserving always, however, the due sense of the absolute subordination of the Son to the Father, as recipient to bestower.[1]

St. Paul was in controversy on many subjects, but it does not appear that there was any dispute at all on the subject of his interpretation of the person of Christ. There is no other interpretation to be discovered in the New Testament. Exactly by what process of argument, or under what influences, St. Paul

[1] St. Paul's doctrine of Christ is to be found in 1 Cor. viii. 6, Rom. i. 3, ix. 5, Phil. ii. 6–11, Col. i, 12–18.

reached this conviction, we can only partially explain. He certainly held that flesh and blood had not revealed it unto him, but God. Also what exactly St. Paul did know or did not know of the contents of our Gospels we cannot estimate. But two things we can say with confidence: first, that no other conception than that which we find in St. Paul fits the facts recorded in the Gospels. Jesus there appears as genuinely and fully man: but out of that genuine manhood, and out of the limitations which belong to proper manhood, there emerges something which is more than human—a claim to speak about God and for God with infallible certitude, a claim to pass judgement on men, and to be in fact their final judge, and a claim on men's faith and allegiance which is exclusive of all other claims. Can it be that such a claim could have been made by a mere man on his fellow men without impious presumption, and that so continuously and so deliberately? On the other hand, could anything exceed the constant dependence of Jesus as the Son upon the Father? Can anything really reconcile this properly divine claim with this absolute sense of dependence, except the conception of a Divine Sonship, which means real Deity but also dependent Deity? One of the great

JESUS AND THE APOSTLES 237

glories of the idea of the Incarnation is that it lifts dependence and submission into the very being of God. In this book we are basing ourselves upon the Gospel story as it is given us in Mark and Luke. It is, we think, obvious that in the Gospel of John, Jesus is represented as claiming to be the Eternal Son of the Father who has come into the world. It is quite contrary to the evidence of that Gospel as a whole to interpret such a phrase as "Before Abraham was, I am" as meant to refer to the pre-existence of the Messiah, the (so-called) "Son of Man" of the Book of Enoch. The pre-existing "Man-Messiah" is an idea foreign to St. John, as to St. Paul: as foreign, it seems, to them as it is to our own minds. But leaving St. John out of our present reckoning, we might still refer to sayings of Jesus in St. Mark and St. Luke, which imply a divine sonship, in a more than Messianic sense. In this book, however, which cannot find space for argument on particular texts, we prefer to depend upon something wider and obvious to all—the general evidence that Jesus is found exercising a kind of authority over man which is properly divine authority, and claiming a kind of faith which God only can properly claim.

The doctrine of the Incarnation of the Eternal

Son of God is, we have said, the only theory which can be found in the New Testament. Some of the books indeed make no theory explicit. But it is explicit in St. Paul, in the Epistle to the Hebrews and in the Gospel and First Epistle of John. Let us set under our eyes the summary Prologue of that Gospel, partly in bare translation, but with such amount of added comment as may make its meaning plainer.

> In the beginning was the Word. [The Word or *Logos* is a Jewish expression. It meant such an utterance of God as " Let there be light "—by which God, as it were, proceeded forth into action. In later days the Jews had come to think of this Word of God almost as a distinct reality, as equivalent to " God in action," just as some of them had come to think of the Divine Wisdom, also, almost as a person. But St. John uses the word *Logos* partly no doubt because it was current all over the Greek world, in which he was now living, as an expression for the Reason or Law or Power in the universe, the immanent God.] In the beginning, then, was the Word, and the Word was with God, and the Word was God. The same was in the beginning with God. All things were made by him ; and without him was not anything made that hath been made. In him was life [he was a living person, and for a certain part of his creation, that is man, he was the principle of reason. Thus the life of man, as distinct from that of the rest of the creation, was free and rational]. The life was the light of men. [But man by his rebelliousness frustrated the

JESUS AND THE APOSTLES 239

purpose of the Light. So it came about that] the Light shineth in the darkness [of sin]; and the darkness apprehended it not [or, "and yet the darkness never mastered it." But the manifestation of the Light became clearer]. There came a man, sent from God, whose name was John [the Baptist, the last of the prophets]; the same came for witness, that he might bear witness to the Light, that all might believe through him. He was not that Light, but came that he might bear witness of the Light. There was the true Light, even the Light which lighteth every man, coming into the world. [That is, Jesus.] He was in the world, and the world was made by him, and the world knew him not. [It failed to recognize him.] He came unto his own, and those that were his own received him not. But as many as received him, to them gave he the right to become children of God, even to them which believe on his name: which were born not of bloods, nor of the will of the flesh, nor of the will of a man [or "husband"], but of God. [This text, as read by many of the early Fathers, was "who, i.e. Jesus, was born, etc." In fact it accurately describes the manner of the birth of Jesus as recounted in the opening chapters of Matthew and Luke; but, if the reading in all our Bibles is right, St. John must be describing the "new birth" of Christians in terms suggestive of that on which their new birth is based, the virgin-birth of Christ, as the New Man;] And [in Jesus] the Word became flesh and dwelt among us, and we beheld his glory, glory as of an only-begotten from a Father, full of grace and truth. . . . For the law was given by Moses, grace and truth came by Jesus Christ. No man hath seen God at any time; God only-begotten, which is in the bosom of the Father, he hath interpreted him.

This is a truly magnificent conception of world development! And therein the person of Jesus, as the eternal Word, or Son, of God, is the beginning and the middle and the end. He was the actor in the whole creation : he was the principle of reason and freedom in man: over his voice, audible in all human consciences, not even sin could triumph : then the voice was made more distinct, when the prophet-messengers of divine revelation bore their witness: but that was only a prelude to the actual incarnation of the Word of God in Jesus, who is God himself in the reality of manhood. Thus in Jesus all the obscure things of the incomprehensible God are translated, as far as practical human needs require, into the intelligible lineaments of a human character. "He that hath seen" Jesus "hath seen the Father." It is obvious that such a cosmic conception of Jesus banishes all narrow conceptions of divine revelation, and all limited ideas of divine redemption. Wilfully to reject Jesus the Christ is, no doubt, to reject God and suffer the penalty of such rejection. But he is not only to be found in

JESUS AND THE APOSTLES 241

the pages of the Gospel: he is the Light which lighteth every man, and he is the principle of rational order in the whole universe of his creation.

3. *The Doctrine of the Spirit in the Church*

This idea of the incarnation connects the historical life of Jesus with the whole *past* of humanity—with the whole progressive disclosure of God in nature and in history. But what connects the historical life of Jesus with the *future* of humanity is the idea of "the Spirit." In one sense the Ascension of Jesus was a conclusion and a climax. There could be nothing beyond that. But in another and deeper sense it was only a fresh beginning. "The things that Jesus began both to do and to teach," he was to go on doing and teaching through his Spirit in the Church which is his body, the organ of his perpetual action. St. John's Gospel gives us in some wonderful chapters (xiv.-xvi.) the last discourses of Jesus to his disciples, and they deal with the new Paraclete—which means "agent" or "representative" of God and of Christ, rather than "Comforter" as it is rendered in our Bible —whom the Father is to send in Christ's name, not so much to supply his absence as to accomplish his presence. For though this "Paraclete" is spoken of as a person and as "another" than Christ, he is so nearly identified with Christ that his coming is also Christ's own return. "I will not leave you orphans, I will come to you." It seems impossible to account for the earliest development of the Christian Church, except on the supposition that substantially such instruction as St. John records was actually given by Christ to his disciples; for the earliest records we have of the Church are full of the enthusiasm of the Spirit. There are difficulties connected with Luke's narrative of the coming of the Spirit at Pentecost which cannot be completely solved. Let us suppose that at points he was under a mistake. But Luke was in close communication for a prolonged period with Philip, one of the Seven, at Cæsarea, and he was in the company of Mnason the "original disciple" at Jerusalem, and he was intimately associated with Mark. We may well accept as the substantial truth his story of the start of the Church in Jerusalem —how the hundred and twenty disciples waited in eager expectation of the promised gift of the Spirit of Power, and how it was poured out upon them and, as it were, intoxicated them, and how then the Church, rapidly growing in num-

JESUS AND THE APOSTLES 243

bers, settled down to its enthusiastic but orderly life, in the consciousness that Jesus, from the height of heaven, was by his Spirit present with them at every point, guiding their every movement and co-operating in their every decision.

But Luke is no philosopher. He relates and does not theorize. We must look to St. Paul's letters for a basis of theory or doctrine concerning the Holy Spirit. We do not indeed find there any connected theorizing or explanation. These letters are occasional compositions for the most part: nor is Paul a writer who defines his conceptions with precision. But we get the basis of a rich doctrine. He gives us a vivid picture of the life of the Church in the cities where he founded it. It is everywhere a community like other active communities, full of complexities and difficulties. But it has an intense corporate consciousness. It is conscious of being possessed, corporately and individually, by the Spirit of Christ. God, that is the Father, and the Lord Jesus Christ, and the Spirit, are each spoken of as distinguishable beings, and as personal, in such phrases as " the grace of Our Lord Jesus Christ, and the love of God, and the fellowship of the Holy Spirit ": " Grieve not the Spirit ": " The Spirit maketh intercession for you ": " There are diversities of gifts, but the same Spirit: and there are diversities of ministries, but the same Lord : and there are diversities of workings, but the same God, who worketh all things in all." (The one text " The Lord is the Spirit," which is constantly quoted to prove that " St. Paul *identified* Christ with the Spirit," is certainly misinterpreted, and ought not to be set against St. Paul's habitual distinction of one from the other.) But though God and Christ and Spirit are distinguished, the transition from one to the other is so rapid and inevitable that their unity is at least as obvious as their distinction. The root idea of the Trinity in God—the One in Three and the Three in One—is already in St. Paul's mind—not explicit, but implicit : and we see how the Name of the One God as St. Paul received it from his fathers', has—as a result of the Christian experience of Jesus, the Son of God, and of the Spirit—become for him the Threefold Name— the name of the Father and of the Son and of the Holy Ghost—still one God.

This is a fascinating subject : but we must not let it lead us beyond bounds. The Church as St. Paul conceives it, or as St. Luke relates its early development, is a quite visible society, having obvious and tangible characteristics.

It is a society bound together by a certain doctrine held in common; it has an authoritative body of governors in the Apostles and those who represent them locally; and it has certain rites of the society, which came to be called "sacraments" or "mysteries"—baptism for initiation, coupled with the laying on of hands, and the common meal, the "breaking of the bread" or "supper of the Lord," which terminated in the eucharistic commemoration of the sacrifice of the death of Christ; and these sacred rites are regarded as divinely given occasions or instruments for the bestowal of the spiritual gifts which the soul of man needs. It must be confessed that in the New Testament we find no trace of an individualistic Christianity. There is no suggestion that membership in Christ is separable from membership in the Church, which is a visible and organized society. The personal endowments of the Christian are linked by the sacraments into the fellowship of the society. Of recent years there has been a great change in the critical attitude towards this idea. Now there is very general readiness to admit that the idea of the organized, sacramental Church is there already in St. Luke and St. Paul. And the function of the Church is to represent in all the world and under all circumstances of success or failure, the true image of human society, struggling and suffering, yet rejoicing in an unconquerable hope. It is the Kingdom of God on earth, living as Jesus taught men to live in the power of his Spirit.

It is thus impossible to think about the Life of Jesus, as the New Testament puts it before us, without recognizing that it refuses to be confined within the limits of the mortal life ending in death. It showed itself, after death, as a life still active from the heavens by the Spirit which is also the Spirit of the Father, in the Church; and again, it is a life which, though it was at a definite moment in history incarnate in Jesus of Nazareth, yet, before this and beyond this, was and is universal and eternal. Such was the conviction which the first disciples of Jesus found themselves constrained to form. Such is the creed in which the Church has found its high mission, however often it has proved itself unworthy of its calling.

4. The Narratives of the Birth of Jesus

Nothing has been said in this little book about the narratives of the birth of Jesus which are found in St. Matthew and St. Luke. It appears that the first preaching of the

JESUS AND THE APOSTLES 247

Apostles was strictly limited to what had fallen within their own experience. Great stress is laid on this principle of personal testimony. Thus, whereas among the grounds on which faith in Jesus is claimed in the New Testament, the fact of his resurrection holds the chief place, no appeal is made to any similar miracle accompanying his birth. We are probably right in drawing the conclusion that it never ought to be made part of the grounds on which faith is claimed. It is with those grounds, which lie in the story of his life and ministry and teaching and death and resurrection, that we have been dealing. It is on those grounds that each man must determine his personal attitude towards Jesus—whether he only bows to him with respect or also worships him on his knees—whether he is to him an historical example only or also the Divine Saviour.

On the other hand, when once men did believe in Jesus, probably before Luke wrote his Gospel, they had heard the account of his Virginal Conception, and it seemed so congruous to what they had come to believe about him— that he was the very Son of God Incarnate and that he was not only true man but new man—that it was welcomed eagerly for truth, and became at once part of the creed of the Church. Thus the fact that Jesus was born of the Virgin Mary, without human father, has down the ages appeared to be inseparable from the faith in the Incarnation and from the faith in the corporal Resurrection. The present writer believes that those who hold that faith, or even are disposed to hold it, will find good grounds for the conclusion that the lovely narrative of St. Luke's early chapters comes from the only source which could make it trustworthy—from Mary herself—not in form but in substance; and that Matthew's narrative rests, as the internal evidence so forcibly suggests, on the witness of Joseph. The attacks made upon these narratives have been vehement and continuous, but they have received reasonable answers. The discussion of them, however, demands more space than is at our disposal. We must be content to leave them for treatment elsewhere, only asking that no one will treat as disproved by loud denials something the grounds of which he has never frankly or fairly examined. When he does come to examine them, he will find them adequate.

CHAPTER VII
EPILOGUE

I HAVE endeavoured to follow out the scheme for the book indicated in the Preface : I have described the conditions, political, social and religious, under which Jesus of Nazareth appeared in Palestine : I have traced his life and ministry, especially as given in St. Mark's and St. Luke's Gospels, down to his crucifixion, with some more detailed account of his teaching : I have endeavoured to estimate the trustworthiness of the narratives, setting aside the idea of verbal infallibility, but affirming the evidences of trustworthiness and of a real inspiration of the writers by a spirit of truth : finally I have sought to trace out how the memories of Jesus' life in the minds of the Apostles, seen in the light of his resurrection and under the experienced inspiration of his Spirit, developed into the Christian creed as we find it in the New Testament, as a whole.

Christianity went out into the world as a

life to be lived, and that the life of a closely organic community, rather than as a theory or a theological creed to be believed. It ought always to present itself to the world primarily as the good life to be lived in human brotherhood. It is lamentable that doctrinal conflicts, about Christ and about the sacraments and about the organization of the Church, have caused it to present to the modern world quite a different aspect. We can therefore easily see the excuses there are for the violent reaction against " dogmatism " and " institutionalism " which possesses the modern mind. But the most misused ideas are apt to contain the most necessary truths. The reaction has been excessive. Ideas in fact are incarnate in institutions; and life cannot really be dissociated from doctrines. In the long run what any society is to become will depend on what it believes, or disbelieves, about the eternal things. Thus, seen justly, Jesus' ethical teaching, and the spirit of catholic brotherhood in the early Church, involved, or were bound up in, specific doctrines about God and man, such as form a connected creed; and Jesus really was, as *Ecce Homo* so rightly insisted, the Founder of an Institution, the New Israel, the Church. The reaction against dogma and the sacramental institutions has been, like all reactions, excessive. " Oh, yet, consider it again ! "

Fifty years ago, under the influence of men like Thomas Huxley, we were asked to believe that the Christian moral standard would persist, though the Christian doctrines had lost their hold. Now it is apparent to almost everyone that this is not so. What is most obviously in question to-day is the moral standard inculcated by Christianity from the first, as it affects alike the life of the individual and the life of the society. It has become apparent that the moral standard will not survive, unless the doctrine is true.

Dr. Edwyn Bevan has just been very forcibly urging upon us that, as the result of many attempts, it must be taken as proved that " if you set out to reconstruct a merely human Jesus behind the documents, you can get nothing with any claim to objective validity." " We are forced to the conclusion that if the Gospel accounts of the words and actions of Jesus . . . falsifies the historical reality, any reconstruction of the real Jesus behind the documents will be too conjectural and arbitrary to make it worth while for men to go on calling themselves his followers." This conclusion, I believe, is true. I believe it is also true, as he suggests, that though we cannot claim infallibility for our records, we can claim that they are "true to the actuality." But the judgement we form on them will never be purely a matter of historical criticism. It depends largely on the state of mind of the critic—on whether he does or does not entertain, as a credible idea, the fundamental thought of God as the Redeemer of mankind.

The Biblical critics, like other specialists, constitute a world apart. Like other bodies of specialists they exaggerate the worth and certainty of their conclusions, and mislead the public—just as the "orthodox economists," or the Liberal advocates of "Science as the Instrument of Necessary Progress," misled the public in Victorian days. They have put forth theory after theory, which have indeed "something in them"—but not all that they put into them. For instance, the theory that the Christianity of the Catholic Church was substantially a product of Hellenism had "something" in it, but it remains true that the Christianity of the New Testament grew substantially on the Jewish, not the Hellenic, root. But so many theories let loose in the air produce in "intelligent," but uncritical, minds a feeling that everything (everything connected with religion, at least) is uncertain, but that meanwhile all theories are interesting. This frame of mind—which hardly even seeks or prays to form decisions or convictions for life—is indeed disastrous. Joseph Conrad's wail—though it is whimsically expressed—represents the truth : " You see, the *belief* is not in me—and without the belief— the brazen, thick-headed, thick-skinned, immovable belief, nothing good can be done." To form and hold convictions, as a basis for life, ought to be every man's aim. We must not be misled by a group of self-confident specialists, whose conclusions we really can, if we will, in great measure test for ourselves. Is the Figure in the Gospels then, Human and Divine, the true record of history ? " Oh, yet, consider it again."

AUTHORITIES

In Chapter I. Dr. Edwyn Bevan's *Environment, Social, Political and Religious, of Israel from Maccabees to Our Lord* (in " a New Commentary on Holy Scripture, including the Apocrypha," S.P.C.K., 1928); Dr. Klausner's *Jesus of Nazareth* (Engl. trans., Allen & Unwin).

In Chapters II and IV. Commentaries in the above volume on St. Mark (Prof. Cuthbert Turner) and St. Luke (Dr. Gore), Latham's *Pastor Pastorum* (Cambridge Press) and Dr. D. S. Cairns' *The Faith that Rebels* (Student Christian Movement).

In Chapter III. Sir John Seeley's *Ecce Homo* (Macmillan); Gore's *Reconstruction of Belief*, Pt. II (Murray).

In Chapter V. R. H. Streeter's *Four Gospels* (Macmillan), Vincent Taylor's *First Draft of St. Luke* (S.P.C.K.). On St. Matthew, see Commentary as above. On St. John, Lord Charnwood's *According to Saint John* (Hodder & Stoughton).

In Chapter VI. Gore's *Reconstruction*, Part III; E. G. Selwyn's *Evidence of the Resurrection* (in Commentary as above), also *The Virgin Birth* in the same volume.

INDEX

Angels, 56, 227
Annas, 26, 162
Apocalypses, 110
Apostles (the Twelve), 59, 86
Ascension (The), 228

Bethsaida, 27, 44
Boanerges, 59, 133
Brethren (of Jesus), 86

Caiaphas, 162
Church (The), 118, 126, 244*, 250
Cæsarea Philippi, 27, 44, 89
Cross (The), 113, 129, 170

David (family of), 43
— (psalm of), 148
Devils, 56
Doublets, 134

Enoch (Book of), 111
Entry (triumphal), 141
Essenes, 35

Fig Tree (miracle of), 143

Galilee, 27, 29, 53, 69, 74, 141, 221, 225
Gethsemane, 158
Gospels, criticism of, 177
— Trustworthiness, 203, 251

Herod, the Great, 23
— Antipas, 27, 52, 88, 166
— Philip, 27

Israel (its vocation), 14
— (political fortunes), 19

Jesus, education, 41
— Baptism, 46
— Temptation, 47
— Early ministry, 51
— In Galilee, 54
— Success and failure, 60
— Teaching, 62, 92
— Use of O.T., 63
— Towards women, 73
— Reformer, 78
— " Extreme," 80
— Ascetic ?, 84
— Poetry of, 92
— Proverbs, 95
— Parables, 96
— Other-worldliness of, 124
— Sternness, 137
— Journeys toward Jerusalem, 132
— Final ministry, 141
— Capture, trials, crucifixion, 160
— Apocalypse, 114, 151
— N.T. doctrine concerning, 231
— Birth narratives, 246
John's Gospel, 200
John Baptist, 37
Joseph (husband of Mary), 42, 248
— of Arimathæa, 163, 174
Josephus, 39
Judas Iscariot, 153

* Here and elsewhere the number given should be understood as only the *first* of several pages.

INDEX

Kingdom of God, 37, 53, 114
Klausner, 28, 149, 170

Lazarus (raising of), 142
Lord's Prayer, 104
Luke's Gospel, 197

Maccabees, 21
Mammon, 62
Mark, 160
— His Gospel, 178, 193
Martha and Mary, 140
Mary (the Mother), 41, 173, 247
Matthew's Gospel, 199
Messiah (ideas of), 108
Meyer (Ed.), 190, 200
Miracles, 47, 56, 182, 209
Moffatt's Bible, 15

Nazareth, 42, 58, 61

Old Testament, 17

Passover, 42, 156
Peter (Confession of), 89
— (Rebuke of), 90
— (Denial), 164
— Gospel of (Apoc.), 223
Pharisees, 22, 31, 148

Pilate, 25, 165
Priests (Chief), 23, 25, 146
Prophets, 16
Psalms of Solomon, 109
Publicans, 30

Q. (Quelle), 79

Resurrection (Evidence), 213

Sadducees, 33, 147
Sanhedrin, 26, 162
Schweitzer, 114
Scribes, 31, 65
Seeley's *Ecce Homo*, 188, 250
Sermon on Mount, 99
Servant of Jehovah, 112, 153
Seventy (Mission of), 134
Son of Man, 54, 112
Spirit (Holy), 46, 241
Synagogues, 32, 61

Temple (Cleansing of), 144
— Guard, 25, 160
Tiberias, 27, 44
Transfiguration (The), 131
Trials (The, of Jesus), 161

Zacchæus, 139
Zealots, 35, 77

www.ingramcontent.com/pod-product-compliance
Lightning Source LLC
Chambersburg PA
CBHW071428150426
43191CB00008B/1076